WHO STOLE PUBLIC SCHOOLS FROM THE PUBLIC?

Voices from the Mount Vernon School District

Claudia L. Edwards

University Press of America,® Inc.
Lanham · Boulder · New York · Toronto · Plymouth, UK

University Press of America,® Inc.
4501 Forbes Boulevard
Suite 200
Lanham, Maryland 20706
UPA Acquisitions Department (301) 459-3366

Estover Road
Plymouth PL6 7PY
United Kingdom

Printed in the United States of America
British Library Cataloging in Publication Information Available

Library of Congress Control Number: 2011925330
ISBN: 978-0-7618-5525-5 (paperback : alk. paper)
eISBN: 978-0-7618-5526-2

Cover photos by Andre' O. Watts

™ The paper used in this publication meets the minimum requirements of American National Standard for Information Sciences—Permanence of Paper for Printed Library Materials, ANSI Z39.48-1992

This book is dedicated to my grandchildren—Joshua, Jillian, Gracellia, and Lyric. May you always have access to quality public education and an engaged public committed to making sure you each have every opportunity to realize your true potential.

There is something about communities where people connect with one another—over and above how rich or poor they are materially, how well educated the adults themselves are, what race or religion they are—that positively affects the education of children.

—*Bowling Alone*
Robert D. Putnam

Contents

Part Four: Voices from Focus Groups

Part Five: From Disenfranchisement to Ownership

Figures and Tables

Figures

Tables

Foreword

Cecil H. Parker was my social studies teacher at Nathan Hale Elementary School in 1958. She was a matronly woman and lived in our neighborhood. Mrs. Parker was the first African American teacher in the city and county where I grew up, and she inspired me to be a historian. Since then, history has been my passion and my life's work. Such is the influence of memorable teachers in great schools.

For most of the twentieth century, Mount Vernon, New York, was a stellar suburban model of fine schools in America. All over America, public schools were local institutions designed to be governed exclusively by local citizens and taxpayers and to provide the finest education possible to the children within the community. I was a beneficiary and proponent of public education in Mount Vernon. For twenty-eight years, I lived in Mount Vernon, taught its pre-kindergarten through high school students, and became its first native son to serve as the high school principal. Then, my journey was not unusual. In small suburban cities, a teacher educated by their schools was an asset. They were proud to see young people come home and teach the next generation. But things have changed.

Who Stole Public Schools from the Public? examines Mount Vernon public schools during the last quarter century. The author's findings are not new revelations, but, until now, they were not well understood. Claudia Edwards has taken full advantage of her intimate knowledge of the community—as a former resident, parent, activist, and now scholar—to explain what has happened not only to Mount Vernon's public schools, but also to the city during its shift to African American political leadership. She surgically dissects the demographic, educational, political, and socioeconomic issues that have eaten away at the great expectations and aspirations of those who sought a new and progressive Mount Vernon shaped in their image.

Dr. Edwards brilliantly revisits the issue of "ownership of" versus "access to" a quality education. The school system that nurtured and facilitated my career in academia gave me access. But ownership of public schools is the essence of political empowerment. As an emerging minority, African Americans were content with access. For most people of color, ownership of public schools has remained "a dream deferred"—a dream for another time and generation. Why hasn't this changed?

This book is a brutally honest examination of how a spirited and vocal generation of activists dedicated to political empowerment and control of public schools were successful in part by their perseverance and inevitably by their most potent allies, the racial and demographic shifts that led to their political victory. But it also examines their post-empowerment failure to transform the local schools in positive and progressive directions. Dr. Edwards provides evidence of how their roles as the "new" political elites hastened the near collapse and demise of the school system. The failure of the new leadership to forge the years of struggle and energy into sweeping system-wide, research-based and tested reforms, as Dr. Edwards correctly asserts, was driven by their "misguided" attempts to manage a broken system versus oversee systemic reform.

Over the past decade, the community of Mount Vernon has discovered what many reform-minded professional educators already knew—that is, that changing schools and educational outcomes requires political courage, perseverance, and new levels of compassion and respect for the students, teachers, and parents within the learning community. As an educator once said, "Real change is real hard." Dr. Edwards argues that the most powerful victory for Black-led communities is not the political one, but the creation of a sustainable, stellar educational experience for their children.

We have waited a long time for a scholarly understanding of what went right and wrong in Mount Vernon. This book provides accurate diagnoses of the problems in public schools in the Mount Vernon School District and similar schools around the country in the early twenty-first century. The prognoses and prescriptions for public schools are most hopeful if they are indeed heeded by local policymakers, citizens and taxpayers.

Who Stole Public Schools from the Public? is mandatory reading not only for Mount Vernon but also communities all over New York State and the nation that are trying to make sense of what happened in the majority of Black-led school districts. It is a courageous look at race, schools, and local politics. It is a primer for those interested in the truth and the reconciliation necessary to move from preoccupations with past and present failures to the creation of new systems of schools truly owned by the public—schools that reflect the community's good sense about what is quality and what is sustainable in their neighborhoods.

Thank you, Dr. Edwards.

Larry H. Spruill, Ph.D.
Mount Vernon City Historian
Morehouse College
Atlanta, Georgia

Preface

Mount Vernon is the place I called home for more than twenty years. During the early 1980s, I was Executive Director of the Housing and Neighborhood Development Institute, a local housing development corporation in Mount Vernon, New York. I led the organization's charge to increase the availability of affordable housing for low- and moderate-income families at a time when Westchester County had one of the highest rates of homelessness in the country. Families were being displaced from nearby municipalities by the clearing of neighborhoods brought on by the federal urban renewal program and by overall gentrification taking place in the New York metropolitan region. I was also among the many residents who fought for increased Black representation on the Board of Education of the Mount Vernon public school district and in public school administration during the 1980s.

The battle for integration of public schools had been won by the 1960s, giving way to the dismantling of de facto segregation that had existed during the early- and mid-twentieth century. Over the next ten years, public schools in Mount Vernon, which had been populated predominately by Whites, began to experience the influx of African American and Latino students. By 1972, African American and Latino students represented the majority of students in all but three schools. Although these two groups combined constituted the *new majority* of students in the Mount Vernon School District (MVSD), and White students had become the *new minority,* the communities from which the new majority came had little influence over policymaking decisions affecting the district.

In addition to being confronted with the challenges our housing clients encountered in keeping their children in school while they struggled to find housing accommodations, I, like many residents, was personally concerned with the state of affairs in the local public school district. I even chose alternative settings for the education of my own children. Out of my growing frustration with the absence of high-performing schools, I became involved in education politics and was one of the founders of Voices of the Electorate. VOTE, as it was called, was a grassroots organization established in the late 1980s to mobilize community support for greater Black representation on the board of education of the MVSD and on the district's administrative team. At the time, the board was controlled by a White political machine led by the Italian Civic Association, the ICA. For more than 30 years, the Black community had been fighting for a greater presence on the school board; I also had great expectations for what could be achieved—if we only had representatives on the board that had an interest in the Black community. Although change was not immediate, by 1999 the fight for equal representation on the school board had been won. For the first time, the board of education was governed by a majority of trustees who represented the Black community. Since then, they, like the new majority of students within the district, have become the new majority on the board.

In the summer of 2007, I returned to Mount Vernon on a research mission. I wanted to discover what had become of this once disenfranchised community and the degree to which the Black community's vision for public schools had been realized. Having emerged from de facto segregation, followed by integration and, more recently, re-segregation, Mount Vernon presented an opportune setting for examining civic capacity and its role in shaping education policy in the aftermath of re-segregation. Many urban centers across the country have gone through the process of re-segregation with the emergence of a new majority. Yet, in spite of this change in the political power base, several Black-led municipalities are noted for not having lived up to the expectations of those who subscribed to the notion that race was at the core of the many inequities confronting the Black community. According to the authors of *Mayors in the Middle*, although some progress has been made, most Black-led communities continue to struggle under conditions of poverty; and their public school systems are in distress.[1]

Homecomings often prompt an uneasy mixture of familiarity and discomfort, and I encountered both upon my return to Mount Vernon. One of the first things I did was to attend a public meeting of the board of education of the MVSD. As I observed the meeting, it became apparent that even though the Black community now had control over the public school district and local government, there were sectors of the public that were as disenfranchised in 2008 as they had been in the 1980s, when Mount Vernon public schools were controlled by the ICA.

The board meeting lasted about two hours and fewer than thirty people attended. Several people from the audience spoke before the board during the period reserved for community responses. The search for a new superintendent was foremost in the minds of the audience that night, and most of their comments revolved around the interview process. It was a provocative, yet civil, session.

At the end of the meeting, I joined a group of residents who had gathered in the halls outside the board room. I recognized one woman from my days as an organizer for VOTE. Speaking on behalf of a group, she expressed the community's distrust over the selection process for the new superintendant by explaining that many people assumed that the board had already "hand-picked their man." I was taken aback when she blurted out that they were convinced that the board, in spite of its majority Black representation, was nothing more than a "Black ICA."

Thus, my journey to discover what the community had to say about its relationship with its public school district had begun. I was in search of answers for what was needed for the public to take greater ownership of its public schools.

I had returned at a time of political flux characterized by an air of uncertainty and a high degree of speculation among the people of Mount Vernon. Many people were preoccupied with the possibility of a change in leadership at city hall and within the MVSD. In addition, there was much talk about growing unrest within the community at large, which had become evident at a recent town meeting. Several incidents of violent crime among youth, including the murders of two Mount Vernon youths in April 2007, had left residents in an uproar. For the first time in recent history, an estimated 1,000 residents from all over the city convened at the Macedonia Baptist Church on May 1, 2007, to voice their concerns about the increase in violence among the city's youth and to demand solutions.[2] It was obvious that change was a concern of many who were poised to see how upcoming events would shape the next chapter in the history of their city.

In less than a month, leaders of the local Democratic Party would hold primary elections for the party's mayoral candidate. Two of Mount Vernon's favorite candidates were seeking the nomination. The incumbent, Mayor Ernest D. Davis, backed by the Democratic Party, was seeking nomination for a fourth term of office. In spite of media accounts of a federal investigation of city hall for alleged misappropriation of funds plus an increase in local violence reflected in gang-related crime statistics, the mayor and his many supporters believed that he deserved another term in office.

Calling for a change in leadership was the Honorable Clinton I. Young, a longtime resident who was a member of the Democratic Party, a former school board trustee, and a sitting representative on the Westchester Board of County Legislators. Young, described by many as an esteemed friend and one-time protégé of the sitting mayor, was challenging the party and its endorsement of the incumbent.

The rhetoric coming from both camps in a Democrat-controlled local government set the stage for a highly contentious race. Among their many differences, Davis and Young had two distinct perspectives on how the school district should be operated. Davis was interested in possessing greater legal control over the district. Specifically, he wanted the appointments of school board trustees to be the prerogative of the mayor. Young, on the other hand, favored having stronger ties between the mayor and the district. Young campaigned as a champion of public education, vowing to use the office of mayor as a bully pulpit to support higher-achieving schools. Rather than the mayor having power to appoint them, Young believed the choice of school board trustees should remain the right of the electorate.

Major changes in leadership were also taking place within the school district. In September 2006, Superintendent Brenda Smith had announced her plans to retire and was poised to vacate her position at the end of school year in June 2007. Characterized as an "insider" and a former resident with strong ties to the community, Smith was a highly regarded professional who had worked tirelessly in the district for over 35 years. She had been named Superintendent in 2002, replacing Ronald Ross, the first Black superintendent to be hired by the new Black political regime.

Although the MVSD experienced significant improvement in student achievement under Superintendent Ross, he had chosen to leave the district. Most people who held an opinion about his administration believed Ross had made a valiant attempt to institute reform. He is credited with improving student performance on state tests, bringing national praise to the district, and helping to rebuild morale. However, many claimed that Ross's management style created a culture of demoralization and disenfranchisement among educators, administrators, and stakeholders in the community.

The board of education soon announced Dr. Welton Sawyer as Smith's successor, effective July 1, 2007. Sawyer had been recruited from the Topeka, Kansas, school district, where he had served as superintendent of schools. He had also served as superintendent of the Manhattan High School District in New York City, where he had built a reputation for being a change agent. Because his area of expertise was secondary education, the board brought him on to address critical problems facing the district, especially at the middle and high school levels.

Controversy had surrounded the selection process during the months leading up to Sawyer's appointment, as some residents were concerned that the process would be usurped by political favoritism, preventing the selection of an individual based on the district's needs. Despite their skepticism about Sawyer's political ties in Mount Vernon, other residents expressed a high level of optimism about the board's appointment. Although there was a sense of loyalty to the previous superintendent, many residents expressed openness to someone new.

In addition to a change in leadership at the level of superintendent, change was taking place on the board of education. Historically, members of the Black church had played a major role in education politics in Mount Vernon. They had not only shaped the education landscape, but also endorsed the election of most of the recent school board trustees, including members of the clergy from three prominent churches. Three trustees, all of whom were Black ministers, were leaving the board that year. One was slated to leave and two others were relocating to churches outside the district and therefore had to resign from the board. There was much uncertainty about who would be elected to these open positions.

With all the turmoil in the city of Mount Vernon at the time this study began, and with no knowledge of who would win and go on to be the next mayor, or who would replace the three members of the board of education who were also members of the Black clergy, I proceeded to interview the study participants and conduct focus groups about civic capacity and public education in the MVSD. In such a politically charged environment, it is a challenge to identify respondents who sufficiently trust a researcher to be willing to participate. Yet in a setting such as this, one cannot underestimate the community's signs of struggle and their need to be heard, even when the Black community holds a majority of seats on the board of education of the school district.

My being an African American woman who had raised two children in Mount Vernon, afforded me the advantage of having had experiences in common with some of the respondents. My status as an *insider* enabled me to make a smooth entry into the community and to approach this work with empathy for—as well as a sense of ease among—various members of the community. In addition, as a former executive of a Fortune 1000 corporate foundation that heavily funded programs in Mount Vernon and a member of one of the largest churches in the city, I was able to draw upon my strong network of professional contacts in governmental and non-governmental entities. These business and personal relationships were very helpful for gaining access to important stakeholders willing to engage in dialogue about the public and its relationship with the school district. My knowledge of the community and my existing relationships resulted in genuine and reciprocal rapport out of which authentic data were collected and mutual growth and knowledge resulted.

This book examines the political dynamics surrounding public education in Mount Vernon, New York, a historically African American urban community that emerged from de facto segregation and integration during the later part of the twentieth century to become one of many urban centers led by African American politicians and administered by African American public officials. It examines the fruition of an African American majority among local public school administrators and officials and their role as the new caretakers of a public school system that had been abandoned by the White middle class by the late 1990s and, to a large extent, by the Black middle class during the period of re-segregation. It also provides a glimpse into what is on the minds of people who remain on the margins of the politics of education and how they may be galvanized to act on behalf of America's urban youth in the early twenty-first century. In the course of my research, approximately one hundred people, including government and elected officials, school teachers and administrators, business leaders and not-for-profit executives, as well as residents from the at-large community, participated in focus groups and in-depth interviews. In their own words, the people of Mount Vernon describe their vision for the district's public schools and provide keen insight into why the community is so disengaged despite Black representation in the school's administration and on the board of education. They also describe the great potential of a community committed to public education and a readiness to be intimately involved in choosing the direction of their public schools in the twenty-first century. Although findings from this research show the tenacity of a people eager to become involved, they also reveal a people ill-equipped to assume ownership of one of its most important public institutions—Mount Vernon's public schools. This book aims to provide community leaders, activists, government and public school administrators, and educators a better understanding of why education reform is slow to take effect in urban communities and what it might take to rekindle the spirit of public ownership of public schools that was once prevalent in America.

Claudia L. Edwards
Tarrytown, New York
September 2010

Acknowledgments

As every author discovers, the making of a book entails more than the tireless efforts of a lone author working in isolation. Much like the course of education, the publication of a book comes by way of many people working toward a goal at every stage of its development. The creation of this book is an example. It came about as a result of various people bringing their unique talents to different tasks over an extended period of time.

This book stems from my research on civic capacity for improving public schools in communities with high concentrations of minority students. It was part of the research requirements that I completed in 2008 as a doctoral candidate at the Graduate School of Education at Fordham University. Several professors at Fordham University guided my initial work, notably, Dr. Barbara Jackson, my mentor and dissertation committee chair; committee member Dr. Toby Tetenbaum; and Dr. Bruce S. Cooper, who encouraged me to publish my research. Dr. Mildred Brown, retired assistant superintendant of the New Rochelle Public School District, also served as a committee member and cheerfully traveled from Florida on many occasions to discuss my research. My research team included Laurel Persons and Brianna Stauffer at the University of Pittsburgh, who facilitated the transcription of over one hundred interview and focus group sessions, and Pamela Kuhens, who identified codes and entered responses into a database.

The Black community of Mount Vernon, New York, has a rich history of struggling for equality alongside Westchester County's White suburban society. I have been fortunate in receiving the guidance and support of its community leaders and members, and I thank them for their perceptiveness with regard to formative aspects of this study. The Reverend Dr. Darin W. Moore, Pastor of the Greater Centennial AME

Zion Church in Mount Vernon, wisely encouraged me to explore a role for the church to improve public schools in the district in the context of the struggle for equality. Professor Larry H. Spruill of Morehouse College had the foresight to preserve the collective memory of that struggle in a recently published history of Mount Vernon entitled, *A Time to Remember: A Portrait of African-American Life in Mount Vernon*. His history of Mount Vernon serves as an anchor for this study, and I gratefully acknowledge his courtesies in allowing me to adapt portions of his book in Chapter 3. Joan P. Horton, a long-time Mount Vernon resident, added to the historical background for this study by sharing her oral history of the community's struggle for equality.

Councilman Yuhanna Edwards (a first cousin to the author) and resident Leonard Goodlowe not only introduced me to many people in the community, but also were instrumental in helping me win their trust. Teachers and administrators from the Mount Vernon School District were especially forthcoming about their triumphs and challenges to mounting education reform. I was reminded of their difficult tasks as educators and am grateful for their insights. Dr. David McCalla, Patricia Lyons, and Akia Shanghi were particularly generous with their time in helping me navigate the district and gain access to important documents.

I especially want to thank the nearly one hundred people of Mount Vernon who participated as interviewees and focus group participants. Our conversations were invaluable for understanding the complexities of making education reform a reality. I was humbled by their openness and thank them for entrusting me with accounts of their personal experiences. By preserving those collective views and experiences, we can continue to develop the civic capacity for education reform at the community level.

I also thank the people at University Press of America for their roles in publishing this book: Associate Editor Brooke Bascietto, Acquisitions Editor Lindsay Macdonald, Manager of Editorial Administration Brian DeRocco, Acquisitions Editor Samantha M. Kirk, and Vice President and Director Judith L. Rothman. Special thanks go to copy editor Donald White who treated my manuscript as a work of art and to Dorothy Albritton, for her work in formatting the final manuscript. Their meticulous attention to detail and thoughtful crafting of the text are evident in the final product.

Finally, much gratitude goes to my family and friends for their unwavering support and love throughout this endeavor. It has been upon their shoulders that I have stood. Thank you for all that you have done and continue to do to enrich my life's journey.

Introduction

Public education is woven into the fabric of American democracy. America has a rich historical legacy of public support for education. Yet, in recent decades, many Americans no longer believe that public schools belong to them. Particularly in urban communities with high concentrations of poor and "minority" groups, we often find a disillusioned public that is missing-in-action on the education home-front. It is as if these communities have been robbed of what had once been their prerogative for public education. What has happened in these communities? And who could have stolen public schools from the public?

This sense of a lack of ownership is not limited to the public schools. It extends to how people feel about many institutions that have been created to serve them. In a search for answers for how to rebuild the important bond between public schools and people in the twenty-first century, Mathews talks about education in the context of a self-governing democracy:

> I think [democracy] is self-government by a sovereign citizenry that exercises its power in communities, statehouses, and the nation's capital. How do citizens get such power? The short answer for me is that we get our power through our ability to join forces and act collectively both with our citizens and through institutions we create to act for us. It follows then, that in order for Americans to be sovereign (that is, to rule themselves), they must be able to direct the institutions they created to serve them. "Directing" in this context means to define the purpose or mission of institutions, not to control their day-to-day activities.
>
> Democracy is not micromanagement. However, if the citizenry can't determine the mission of institutions such as public schools, self-rule is seriously undermined.[1]

Mathews argues that public schools grow out of the broad objectives of democracy and that public ownership of public schools extends far beyond the parents of children who attend public schools. It is the responsibility of the entire public, not just parents, to ensure that public schools reflect the vision of their community. He proposes that a public must exist before it can act on behalf of public education, and he develops a case for *public building* that is based on acts done by the public—for itself. Mathews conceptualizes the public and its capacity to be a dynamic force—one that creates itself in the process of doing its work.[2]

Although programs to reform public education have been tried in urban schools over the last three decades, not one of them has changed the connection of family and community poverty with low academic achievement.[3] In spite of brave attempts by new superintendents to launch reform efforts, educators are consistently frustrated by unchanged patterns of low student achievement and growing dissatisfaction on the part of the public. Although there are school districts that have shown significant improvements, there are very few examples of any that have sustained reform beyond the tenure of a sitting superintendent or the life of a grant-initiated or sponsored reform program. In cases where success stories do exist, they are typically found among elementary schools with extraordinary principals, an involved teaching staff, and an engaged community.

This is not to suggest that reform efforts should be discontinued or that none has been effective. The significant gains resulting from the *Success for All* model developed by Johns Hopkins University cannot be overlooked. Nor can the work of Comer and his School Development Program, which is acclaimed by many educators as among the most successful reform efforts.

Civic Capacity as a Framework for Education Reform

To explore how to improve public schools in poor urban communities, we must look elsewhere and consider the issue of public engagement with education. Stone and his colleagues find that education policy is not created in a political vacuum.[4] Its formulation occurs within a broader set of existing relationships within and among local, state, and federal political environments. Although finance has a major impact on education quality, good funding, in and of itself, is no guarantee of sustained improvement in academic achievement. They point out that, given the nature of American education politics, it is unlikely that education reform for urban centers will result from a shift in education policy:

> In a predominantly suburban nation, political reality runs against the likelihood that broad support can be organized around a program of redistribution that favors city schools. Putting substantially more money into urban schools at the expense of suburban schools (or into schools of color at the expense of White ones or into lower-income schools over higher-income ones) is, as one pair of authors observed, 'politically inconceivable.'[5]

Many programs seek to transform failing schools through engaging significant numbers of parents.[6] They focus on changing a school's culture, including the quality of relationships among educators, parents, and children, as well as the educational outcomes of its students. Although successful, traditional methods of involvement have been limited to treating parents of children attending school as consumers of education.[7]

Over the last decade, a new school of thought has emerged in response to the need to build important relationships between public schools and the community—especially parents. Public engagement, as described by Friedman, et al., involves building community support for public education by defining meaningful ways to get all citizens more actively involved in educating children. It focuses on the political aspects of education reform in two ways that recognize the need for a collective response to education reform: first, by expanding outreach beyond parents to include representation from all segments of the community; and second, by changing the public from *consumers* into *owners* and *guardians* of public education.[8]

This need for public engagement comes at a time in American history when the nation has suffered a major erosion of its social capital. In *Bowling Alone*, Robert Putnam explores the degree to which Americans have withdrawn from those civic activities which have made America strong. In tracing the trends that describe this decline in social capital, Putnam reports that in the last quarter of the twentieth century citizen participation in civic affairs declined by one-third.[9]

Civic Capacity and Ownership of Public Schools

The idea of ownership of public schools is based on the premise that all public institutions belong to the public and were established by the public to achieve desirable public outcomes. That is, every citizen who lives under our democratic society is the legitimate owner of all public institutions, including public schools. This is not to suggest citizens want to or should be involved in the day-to-day operations. But it does suggest that members of a community should take the lead in shaping the vision for their schools—a vision that represents their shared beliefs about preparing children for productive citizenship in our democratic society. Since ownership does not come without responsibility, the entire community is accountable for making sure high-performing schools with adequate resources are available for all its children.

We often see this sense of ownership of public schools in communities with high concentrations of the wealthy and middle-class families. These families often move into communities with public school districts having a reputation for high-quality public schools, heavily funded by local property taxes, leveraged government subsidies, and private funding. They elect to pay high premiums for living in these communities with the expectation that ownership is an unquestionable entitlement.

Yet this phenomenon of *ownership* is seldom apparent in urban communities with high concentrations of minority groups. We find many examples of communities where African Americans have gained the political leverage to become the new *majority,* controlling important governmental and school district posts, both elected and appointed. In spite of these victories, the vast majority of the public in many Black-led school districts have not performed as owners of their local public schools. In spite of their new political standing, the public continues to show behaviors typical of disenfranchisement—sitting on the sidelines of education politics, either unable or unwilling to build and sustain important coalitions needed to build high quality, high-performing schools. To understand this phenomenon, it is important to revisit the historical relationship between the public and its public schools. During twentieth century reform efforts to professionalize public education and move toward a more equitable and uniform American universal public education system, education policy resulted in the shifting of the public's political standing as *owners* of public education to that of *recipients or consumers*. In addition, interpretations of education policy resulted in the narrowing of ownership rights to public education from the *general public* to *parents of children attending public schools*. Although American history is rich with evidence of a highly motivated public actively involved in shaping the Republic—and in particular shaping its local schools[10]—at the present, and in the recent past there are many communities with a *public* unaware of this historical legacy. Today, we often find—devoid of that fervor for public schools they once possessed—a disillusioned citizenry who decline to report for duty in the battle for better schools. This is too often the case in urban communities with high concentrations of poor and minority groups. This situation prompted the title of this book: *Who Stole Public Schools from the Public?*

The struggle for ownership of public schools is not a major theme of African American history in this country. Even the fight for Civil Rights and the end of government-sponsored segregation did not focus significantly on such "ownership" rights for African Americans. It centered on the right of African Americans to have "access" to an equitable education system—something they had been systematically denied throughout American history.[11] Even segregated public schools in the south were not established as a result of choice by an empowered African American public, but out of circumstances mandated by the Jim Crow laws. Twentieth century reform efforts resulted in a paradigm shift that gave African Americans increased access to public schools. It did not, however, result in their gaining greater ownership or control of those schools. Ownership of American public schools by African Americans has almost never existed. When dealing with the question of who stole public schools from the public, one is led to wonder how something can be stolen from those who never really possessed it.

Exploring Civic Capacity in a Black-led City

To better understand this phenomenon and the apparent absence of public will in Black-led communities, this book explores causes for this disconnect in the instance of Mount Vernon, New York. It examines under what conditions the diverse population of Mount Vernon could take greater ownership of their public schools by coming together to improve the performance of public schools in the Mount Vernon School District. In attempting to measure the public's readiness to take its place as owners of their local school district, it focuses on four lines of inquiry: first, the extent to which there was a shared belief that the people of Mount Vernon valued the institution of public education; second, the extent to which the public believed there were major problems within the school district that needed immediate attention; third, the extent to which the public valued the idea of building a coalition of support for public education; and fourth, what barriers had to be overcome to build and sustain broad-based public support for public education.

Using qualitative research methods, the author conducted 78 in-depth interviews and five focus groups to examine the extent to which the political environment in the current Black-led municipality of Mount Vernon is conducive to building civic capacity with an aim toward developing a community vision for its local schools. Building on the work of Stone,[12] this book examines why the public is disconnected from its public schools and how it can become a sustaining, powerful force engaged in securing quality education for all children. Qualitative research methods used in this study provided the flexibility needed for an in-depth understanding of the public and its perceived relationship with its public schools. They also provided the opportunity to gain important insights into what conditions might enable a collective response to occur.

Several mechanisms were put in place to assure the accuracy and completeness of the data collected through the interviews and focus groups and the validity of the findings. Interviews and focus groups were audio-recorded, and transcripts of the audio files were prepared by services at the University of Pennsylvania, allowing for independent documentation of the information collected. In addition, an independent research consultant identified codes and input responses into a statistical database. The use of these independent sources to capture and organize the data served to reduce the potential for biased analyses and findings on the part of the author.

Finally, by going directly to the public in Mount Vernon to hear their views on their relationship with the local school district, the present study attempts to move beyond the traditional methods for engaging parents in public schools by examining meaningful ways in which the public in a community with a high concentration of African American and Latino residents, many of whom are poor, can become galvanized to address the educational needs of their children. The findings presented in this book address how increased civic capacity may be achieved in the political context within which Mount Vernon schools operate. They are intended to provide insights that may be of value to stakeholders who are interested in understanding why the public in Mount Vernon has been disengaged in spite of the black community's success in gaining political control within the community, as well as to stakeholders who are interested in exploring civic capacity as a strategy to build public support for improving local public schools.

Acronyms and Abbreviations

CEPAA	Coalition for the Empowerment of People of African Ancestry
ELA	English Language Arts
GED	General Educational Development (also Certificate of General Educational Development)
ICA	Italian Civic Association
MOM	Mothers of Mount Vernon
MVSD	Mount Vernon School District
NAACP	National Association for the Advancement of Colored People
NCES	National Center for Education Statistics
NCLB	No Child Left Behind
POAD	People of African Descent
PTA	Parent-Teacher Association
SAT	Scholastic Aptitude Test
SRP	State Reference Point
UBC	United Black Clergy
VOTE	Voices of the Electorate

Part One

Public Engagement with Education in America

Chapter 1

Themes of Public Engagement in Historical Perspective

From the seventeenth through the nineteenth centuries, the evolution of public education in America was woven into the fabric of American democracy. It was shaped by an engaged public who felt a sense of ownership of their local schools.[1] The public played a significant role in ensuring that their local schools reflected the values and ideals people envisioned for their communities. Examples of an engaged public in the eighteenth century vividly illustrate the public's role in formulating the first schools in colonial America. Even prior to 1860, American history reflects a strong public will to create its ideal society.

Early pioneers operated under the assumption that public schools belonged to the public and that schools were established by the public to achieve its vision for their children's education. The public were not viewed simply as voters or consumers, but as people using their collective capacities in a variety of ways to achieve a common good.[2] Public involvement, particularly during the eighteenth and nineteenth centuries, demonstrates what an engaged public can achieve through collective action. The following survey of selected examples from the American experience provides insights into the potential for a modern public to strengthen public education, particularly in Black-led communities.

The Public's Early Capacity to Build Informal Networks

The expansion of the early American colonies was a result of the public working together to survive the elements of a new and foreign environment and, despite scarce resources, building schools in order to meet the needs of the public. Focusing on the exemplary role people in community after community played in the establishment of the first communities in Alabama and the Southwest, David Mathews describes how the early settlers in Claiborne, Alabama worked together to construct a wooden staircase of 365 steps to reach the location upon which the settlement was built—a bluff 365 feet above the Alabama River. Merchants, farmers, immigrant laborers, slaves, free Blacks, and poor Whites all helped to build the staircase in an effort to gain access to their settlement. This example demonstrates how social settings can profoundly affect public life. People found many legitimate reasons to form associations—from sharing in the ritual for preserving meat for the winter, to celebrating hog-killing day.[3]

Other assemblies were held that combined families with larger civic components. For example, camp meetings held on church grounds drew people not only from different congregations, but also from nearby states who traveled more than 100 miles to visit and meet old acquaintances. These meetings reflected the democratic spirit that permeated frontier politics. They affirmed the freedom and power of ordinary people and promoted a public awareness of important issues. Further, these informal associations paved the way for other forms of cooperation and, more explicitly, political gatherings. Public hearings were held to discuss issues and come to consensus on action. The gatherings resulted in the building of roads, the organization of businesses, and the raising of armies.[4]

The Public as Community Builders

Mobile, Alabama, which, by 1819, had evolved from a sixteenth century French fort to a thriving city, offers an example of citizens who built institutions to support their way of life. Once the city received its charter and established a legislative government, new settlers, especially families, began to migrate to the area. Settlers organized associations to provide a multitude of services, including fire-fighting and other emergency help and meeting sanitation needs. Once the most basic living conditions were established, the settlers engaged in what Mathews refers to as *community building*, in which people cooperated to further enhance their community by building public institutions such as roads, shops, courthouses, and churches. People were involved in civic action, because they shared an interest in creating a quality of life conducive to their moral, social, and political values. Public life was energetic yet deferential; people participated freely, as societal engagement was presumed to be a natural aspect of everyday life.

Spontaneous community building was prevalent throughout the Southwestern region of North America. Mathews' study of Alabama provides just one example of the type of public engagement that took place throughout the New World.[5] Today, Alabama offers an example of one of the greatest contradictions in history. With slavery thriving as an important institution in the state, citizens in Alabama were determined to maintain their right to institute slavery in a society they defined as free.[6]

Education and Self-Government

In addition to community building, settlers in the Southwest, as in the rest of the country, were committed to self-government; and education was viewed as paramount for a citizenry determined to govern themselves. Schools were among the first institutions that settlers built in their new land.

Alabamians built schools in ways similar to the way they built other public institutions. The public would identify social problems they believed could be alleviated by institutions of education, and then would collectively plan the formation of schools. The first schools were often initiated by parents with the support of people in their local settlements. Typically, one family out of a small group of pioneers would offer a room in their cabin for teaching children. Children in homes where instruction was not available would join their neighbors. These early schools eventually expanded to become community schools. For example, the first school in Clarke County, which apparently started in the home of Caleb Moncrief, offered schooling to young children in the area. Neighborhoods joined forces to build separate structures for a primary school and a Sunday school. The primary school served the area and became an educational institution that benefitted the community for many years.

The public also rallied to raise financial support and resources for their schools. Neighbors formed associations and raised the dollars needed to erect buildings, and then maintain ongoing operations. Community associations for education differed as much as the communities in which they were formed and reflected the different needs, values, and life circumstances of each particular community.[7]

Public Ownership of Schools in Colonial America

Many schools in colonial America had religious roots.[8] Practically all of the early settlers came from a land where people practiced some form of the Protestant faith. They were people who fled England largely to avoid religious persecution. As a result, the first schools in America were the fruits of the Protestant revolts in Europe.[9] Much of the curriculum focused on teaching children how to read the Bible. This was particularly true of French Huguenots who settled in the Carolinas; Calvinistic Dutch in New Amsterdam; Scotch and Scotch-Irish Presbyterians in New Jersey and along the Allegheny Mountain ridges; Baptists and Methodists in Eastern Pennsylvania; and English Quakers in Philadelphia. Although there were different types of education taking place across early colonial America, a consistent characteristic was the role of the public.[10]

These arrangements meant that family wealth, race, and gender influenced the level of education that was available in America in the late eighteenth and early nineteenth centuries. The public who had a say in education—typically White male property owners—believed it appropriate for education to remain the prerogative of families and the church. This was evidenced in the significant differences in schooling that emerged among various sections of the country. For example, in the South, education was limited to the children of large plantation owners who dominated the region politically. They hired tutors to teach their sons basic academic skills, social graces, and slave management. They instructed their daughters how to be gracious hostesses. Teaching slaves to read was illegal.[11]

In the Middle Colonies, including New York, Pennsylvania, New Jersey, and Delaware, church-sponsored schools were established in local communities where heavy emphasis was placed on students maintaining their parents' native languages and on practicing their respective religious beliefs. For example, the Dutch Reform Church set up schools in New York; and in Pennsylvania, Quakers sponsored schools for children in their community. Each group taught its unique ideology. Despite the lack of uniformity, quality, or equity in distribution of educational resources, and the fact that many groups were excluded from having access to education, this mode of education became the prototype for most American public education in the eighteenth century.[12]

The Will to Sustain Local Control

The establishment of town meetings by early inhabitants during the seventeenth century was a distinctive mode of self-government.[13] These forums survived well into the nineteenth century and served as the foundation upon which the United States Constitution was built. As the tradition of public assemblies continued to spread throughout the country, such gatherings also served as a forum for debates about education. Such gatherings were at the heart of thirty-nine years of public resistance to the adoption of the universal education system first proposed in 1778 by Thomas Jefferson. In 1818, Jefferson charged that his plan was foiled by the strong political will of people in their local communities.[14]

Having won independence from Great Britain in 1783, much lay ahead for the citizenry to build a nation out of 13 former colonies. Many believed that education could play a crucial role in bringing together this very heterogeneous society. In spite of popular public opinion favoring locally controlled schools, famous political leaders during that era, notably Thomas Jefferson, Benjamin Rush, and Noah Webster, were concerned with the uneven nature of schooling throughout the country. Specifically, they were concerned about the extent to which the current mode of education would prepare the next generation to safeguard the young Republic. Jefferson, Rush, and Webster believed schools should not only be more widespread, but also more systemic and publicly supervised.[15]

Despite differences among these three leaders, they each believed the only solution to avoiding anarchy was to create a representative form of government in which the general will of the people prevailed, one that was articulated by the best men in society.[16] An educated citizenry was essential to protect the liberty for which the Revolution had been fought and to uphold the fragile balance between liberty and order. It was believed that education could play a critical role by preparing men to vote wisely and women to train their sons properly.[17]

Although there were calls for statewide educational systems from some of the most prominent founding fathers, the public remained steadfast in its support of locally-controlled schools. Schooling for children in America, through the first thirty years of the nineteenth century, remained unequal, inequitable, and solidly in the domain of local control. Although eighteenth century contributions to the educational debate were significant, their concepts never went much beyond the realm of theory. In spite of the slow progress made, eighteenth century reformers are credited with laying the groundwork for nineteenth century advocates of universal education.[18]

A New and Robust Public: The Urban Wage Earner

New demands for education emerged from the American labor movement, which began in 1827 in Philadelphia. Eighteenth century America was predominantly comprised of rural areas and small towns. After the Revolution, America experienced significant economic growth and expansion. The influx of new immigrants, the advent of new inventions, and mass migrations from rural to urban centers resulted in the transformation of public life. People lived and worked in urban centers across America and drew their earnings from wages as opposed to toiling the land. Economic hardship was an incentive for the eventual launch of the American labor movement with the establishment of the Mechanics' Union of Trade Associations. This union was an alliance of fifteen trade associations that joined ranks to respond to poor conditions in America's workplaces. This alliance was the first of its kind where wage earners from across multiple occupations banded together to demand improved working conditions.[19]

In addition to joining forces for economic reasons, this organization was the first trade association to use its combined might to form a political party: the Workingmen's Party. This political arm was established to address certain social conditions that could not be met through economic methods. As oppressed people, downtrodden by inequalities in the workplace, laborers were inspired by the promise of liberty for which the new Republic, at least in principle, stood. This period in America coincided with the "world's egalitarian age; and in America it witnessed the 'rise of the common man.'"[20] Along with similar affiliates in Boston and New York, the Workingmen's Party, in the summer of 1828, embarked on what was to become the most symbolic and significant event of any labor movement in American history—the election of their candidate for the president of the Republic, Andrew Jackson. The political platform endorsed by the movement won the hearts and minds of the electorate, who used their collective power to deliver victory for their chosen candidate to hold the highest office in the nation.

Free school was at the time only available to the poor.[21] The Workingmen's Party believed this to be in direct contradiction to the nation's claims of liberty and democracy:

> 'Free equal, practical, nonsectarian republican' education became a shibboleth around which rallied the new hosts of labor. They displayed that touching faith to which Americans as a people have been always prone: that a single reform, whether manhood suffrage, free schools, free homesteads, free silver, the single tax, may prove at long last a magical panacea.[22]

Labor Attitudes on Universal Education

Representatives of the Workingmen's Party concerned about education established a committee to investigate the state of education throughout Pennsylvania. The committee found little support for public education except in Philadelphia, Lancaster, and Pittsburgh. It also found many disparities in the operation of charity schools throughout the state. They charged that private individuals were spending government monies to provide less than quality education for the poor. Charity schools, in their opinion, offered limited curriculum and created a loss of pride among parents. They believed government monies were being used primarily to support colleges and universities, which exclusively benefited the rich. Not offering education at younger ages, the workers argued, blocked access to institutions of higher education for children of the working class. Unlike the rich, workers had no means to prepare their children for the academic rigor of higher education.

The New York Workingmen's Party believed that the existence of charity schools and the lack of funding for schooling perpetuated the social and economic class distinctions within American society. They argued that the lack of education kept working men ignorant of their rights, making them vulnerable to exploitation by the privileged. Workers also felt that common schooling was essential to the protection of their rights and necessary for the equal exercise of power in a democratic society.[23] Although much of the literature credits Horace Mann and Henry Barnard for establishing America's free school system, documentation of the worker's movement indicates that America's free school system was almost wholly the result of the unbending agitation of the wage earner—this new robust public rooted in America's urban centers.[24]

Resilience in the Quest for Ownership of Public Schools

Horace Mann played a significant role in advancing the call for universal education during the twentieth century. In spite of much resistance, local control for education gave way to a more centralized system with greater governmental influence. As a result, at least in theory, the business of setting policies and practices for schools was greatly influenced by professionals and less so by parents and local citizens. Following diminished local control of schools, a rejuvenated public emerged in the mid-twentieth century.

Dr. Martin Luther King, Jr. and the many people who participated in the Civil Rights Movement joined the long legacy of an American public who stood up to reclaim public education as the prerogative of the common people. The basis upon which the Civil Rights Movement was launched was, in part, the demand by the American people for the immediate desegregation of America's public institutions, which had been delayed for nearly ten years.[25] For years, federal law permitted states to uphold segregation laws based on race. After more than twenty years of battle, the Supreme Court struck down state authorization of segregation in public schools in the 1954 landmark decision, *Brown v. Board of Education of Topeka,* thereby prompting the desegregation of public schools throughout the United States.

Brown v. Board of Education represents a paradigm shift in public education, one in which little people did big things. The impetus behind this landmark case originated from several lawsuits initiated by parents—common everyday people who were frustrated with the inequitable conditions in their local public schools. Early cases that led to the ultimate decision to end segregation chronicle the story of families who stepped forward in spite of the threat of retaliation. In the face of retribution, these parents dared to hold their local officials accountable for denying African Americans the right to full access to public education. These small individual acts of public engagement evolved into a multiracial national movement that ultimately changed the face of public schools in America.[26]

The period leading up to *Brown v. Board of Education* can be viewed as a period of total public engagement. The National Association for the Advancement of Colored People (NAACP) Legal Defense Fund, the

Urban League, religious groups from all denominations, education professionals, and a cross-section of people from community groups throughout the country, all worked together to affect change in public education. This success was a result of the tenacity of people who claimed full ownership of the institution of public education.

Chapter 2

The Elusiveness of Education Reform

According to an old African saying, "If you want to know the condition of the village, listen to the footsteps and sounds of the children at play." If we were to apply this axiom to measure the condition of public education in the United States at the outset of the twenty-first century, an observer standing outside one of America's urban middle schools or high schools would see that these "villages" are in distress. In *Urban Sanctuaries,* M. W. McLaughlin and colleagues listened to the voices of young people living under devastating conditions in urban areas and noted how, with the help of youth organizations, many students have managed to survive adolescence and gone on to become productive members of society. The authors weave a compelling story of hope in spite of the belief that America has abandoned its urban youth. They challenge the stereotypical mindset that frames society's perceptions of the future of young people in urban communities:

> Americans looking at the young people who live in U.S. inner cities are often overwhelmed by feelings of futility, desperation, and anger. Educated primarily by newspapers' chronicles of inner-city desperation, television's snapshots of the fury and loneliness in urban ghettos, and Hollywood's movies of gangs and life in the "hood," many Americans of all ethnic and economic groups have concluded that little can be done to alter the bleak future of inner-city adolescents.
>
> A frightening number of inner-city youth share this hopeless view of their future, and their voices of despair embody the inner city for

many who live both inside and outside its confines: "You don't plan your future; you just take it as it comes. Life's a constant struggle 'cuz you can't count on anything. You don't know for sure what's even gonna happen the next day. You can get shot walkin' down the street.

"You get more respect for carryin' a Uzi than for going to school. Ain't nobody gonna cheer you on with 'I hope you do well, go to college.'"[1]

Although education is hailed as the primary vehicle for preparing America's children, it has fallen short on its promise to our most vulnerable populations—urban youth trapped in segregated, underfunded schools. These children are more than twice as likely to attend schools in high poverty districts of East St. Louis, Illinois; Detroit, Michigan; Camden, New Jersey; Atlanta, Georgia; and Cleveland and Dayton, Ohio. Schools in urban areas are increasingly segregated, and have high enrollments of African American and Latino students.[2] In these communities, more than four out of ten students are poor. Although their needs are great, these children tend to have far less of the vital resources they need to achieve academic success. They are less likely to have teachers educated specifically in the subjects they teach. These students experience the effects of high turnover among teachers in their schools, making it difficult for students to establish the bonding relationships that are so critical to education.[3]

Students in non-urban school districts are fifty percent more likely than urban students to achieve at, or above, basic levels in reading, math, and science. This performance gap is due, in large part, to social and economic problems, such as poverty and racial discrimination. These factors fall especially hard on inner-city children and are, to a large extent, outside the control of the schools. But low performance among minority students is not solely attributable to the low-income and minority status of these populations. White students in central cities perform as well as their counterparts across the nation on SAT scores. African American students in large cities, on the other hand, score substantially lower than their national counterparts. For example, 46 percent of rural and suburban students in high-poverty schools score at the basic level in reading, in comparison with 23 percent in high-poverty urban schools. In math, the rates are nearly twice as high with 61 percent of non-urban students in high-poverty schools achieving at the basic level compared to

33 percent in high-poverty urban schools. In science, the rates are 56 percent compared with 31 percent.[4]

Re-segregation: A Twenty-first Century Phenomenon

Segregated public school districts are now commonplace for poor Black and Latino urban youth. As middle class families have chosen alternative settings for their children's education, we have witnessed erosion of once-integrated communities and re-segregation of America's public schools. This twenty-first century phenomenon has left increasing proportions of poor urban children trapped in inequitable, segregated public schools that have been abandoned by the White middle class and even, to a large extent, by the Black middle class.

Patterns of re-segregation surfaced during the early 1990s. For the first time since the landmark decision of *Brown v. Board of Education of Topeka* in 1954, segregation of African American students increased significantly and the degree of segregation has been described in quantitative terms. Intensely segregated schools are defined as having 10 percent or fewer White students; and apartheid schools are described as having 99 to 100 percent African American student enrollment.

Between 1991 and 2003, the percent of African American students attending majority non-White schools increased in all regions across the country from 66 percent to 73 percent. For example, during that period, the number of African Americans in schools with 0 percent to 10 percent White-student enrollment increased nationally from 34 percent to 38 percent and grew most rapidly in the Border States, from 33 percent to 42 percent. In 2003, the South and West had the lowest proportions of African Americans in intensely segregated schools. Further, these regions saw an increase of 32 percent compared to 30 percent in 1991. The rates in the Northeast and Midwest increased to 51 percent and 46 percent respectively.

With regard to extreme segregation, the Midwest had the largest concentration of African Americans attending *apartheid schools,* where they represented 99 percent to 100 percent of the student population. These students represented 26 percent of the entire student population in the region. The Northeast followed suit with 23 percent of African American students attending apartheid schools. In contrast, the South (12 percent) and the West (11 percent) were the two regions with the lowest proportions of African American students enrolled in apartheid schools.[5]

Segregation patterns for Latino students were even starker than those of African Americans. For example, in the West, where large numbers of Latinos are concentrated, 81 percent are in schools with high concentrations of non-White students. In the Northeast and South, 78 percent of Latinos attend schools with high concentrations of non-White students. In the West, 39 percent of Latinos attend intensely segregated minority schools with 90 percent to 100 percent minority-student enrollment; and 12 percent attend apartheid schools with 99 percent to 100 percent minority-student enrollment. In the Northeast, 44 percent were enrolled in intensely segregated schools and 15 percent were enrolled in apartheid schools. In the South, where high concentrations of Latinos also reside, an estimated 40 percent of Latino students attend intensely segregated schools and 10 percent attend apartheid schools. In each of these cases, levels of segregation for Latinos are higher than or equal to the levels experienced by African American students.[6]

Integration levels have dropped to a three-decade low. Across the nation, nearly 75 percent of African American and Latino students now attend predominantly minority schools. Nearly 2 million African American and Latino students in the Northeast and Midwest attend apartheid schools.[7]

One of the most disheartening experiences for people who grew up during the Civil Rights Movement is to visit public schools today that bear the names of Martin Luther King, Jr., Thurgood Marshall, or other leaders who fought for integration. Kozol describes the shame these leaders would feel if they were alive to witness how many of the schools bearing their names have become institutions of re-segregation. They would be even more disheartened to know that some of these schools exist in racially mixed areas. For example, Kozol describes a neighborhood in Seattle, where 50 percent of the families are White, but 95 percent of the public school students are students of color; and where clusters of White parents wait near their neighborhood schools for buses that take their children to and from other schools with predominantly White enrollments.[8]

Martin Luther King, Jr. School in New York City is another stark example of intentional re-segregation. As opposed to being located in a deeply segregated low-income community, this school is in an upper middle-class White neighborhood in Manhattan, less than a block from Lincoln Center. When the school opened in 1975, it offered the promise to integrate a school in a heavily diverse community; in reality, it became a "dumping ground" for African American and Latino students. Furthermore, the school remains a symbol dramatizing some of the problems of the nation.[9]

These schools are not isolated examples of segregated schools in selected communities. They represent a growing pattern that has become typical of urban communities across the country. For example, in Chicago, 87 percent of public school enrollment is African American or Hispanic. In Washington, DC, 94 percent of the students enrolled are minority. In St. Louis, 82 percent are minority students. Although New York City had an overall minority student enrollment level of 78 percent, high schools in the outer boroughs like the Bronx had, in most cases, high school enrollments of up to 95 percent minority students.[10]

The number of African American and Latino students enrolled in the nation's public schools increased by 5.8 million since the Civil Rights Movement, while enrollment among White students declined by nearly the same amount—5.6 million. This shift in enrollment is due to a combination of factors, including different birth rates and a significant increase in immigration. For example, the Latino population, estimated at 2 million in 1968, has grown over a thirty-year period to 6.9 million, representing a growth rate of 245 percent.[11]

The Emergence of Segregated Schools in Suburban Communities

Evidence of re-segregated schools is not only surfacing in urban communities. It is even more pronounced in suburban communities. In *A Multiracial Society with Segregated Schools: Are We Losing the Dream?*, the authors describe increased patterns of imbalanced racial enrollment and segregation in American public schools in the year 2000. They cite the growing trend toward re-segregation occurring in suburban schools. For example, in 1967 some of the nation's largest suburban systems, which had been virtually all White, began to experience an influx of minority families that moved to the suburbs in search of a higher quality of life for their family and better schools for their children. Initially, schools with predominately White students experienced a gradual increase of minority students. However, by the late 1960s, patterns of segregation emerged. For example, in Roosevelt, on New York's Long Island, nearly 100 percent of students enrolled at the high school were African American or

Hispanic. In contrast, at Plainview High, a twenty-minute drive away, African American and Latino enrollment was 1 percent, while White enrollment was 97 percent.[12]

The Tragedy of Unequal Education

Racial segregation is not only about race, but also about the inequities that occur as a result of racism. The struggle to end segregation was not motivated by a desire to have African American children sit next to White children. There was the strong belief that schools with large White enrollments offered better opportunities on a variety of levels. It was believed that these schools offered greater competition, more demanding courses, and better facilities and equipment, and also produced higher levels of academic achievement and graduation rates. Research showing the correlation between race, segregation, and poverty provides evidence of a syndrome of inequities that shape schooling of America's poor and minority students in schools with high concentrations of poverty.[13] These schools have less qualified, less experienced teachers, lower levels of peer group competition, and higher turnover rates among teachers and administrators. In addition, school administrators in these schools are burdened with higher costs for education based on the many special needs associated with children living in poverty.[14]

The consequences of unequal education have a significant impact on the next generation of citizens. Because employment and income are so closely linked to education in this information age, postsecondary education is essential for America's youth. With the decline of well-paying manufacturing jobs that require less education, high school graduates with no college or technical training will find it increasingly difficult to compete in the global economy. Nearly half of the high schools in America's largest cities were graduating less than half of their students in the mid-1990s and these schools were predominantly segregated, minority schools.[15]

What is so troubling about the plight of young people trapped in segregated schools is that many of them live in communities with an *unengaged public*, ill-equipped with the political savvy needed to participate as owners of public schools to demand greater accountability. Even in cases where minority groups have seized political control over their local communities, those gains have not always produced tangible improvements for the broader public. What we have learned about the new political order in these re-segregated school districts is that while minority groups have successfully built the coalitions needed to increase their representation in key governmental positions and on local public school boards, such coalitions have not been successful in sustaining themselves over time. Nor have they had success in claiming ownership of schools and holding their elected officials accountable for the quality of schools.[15] As a result, America's promise to provide all children an equitable public education continues to be elusive for the vast majority of African American and Latino youth attending re-segregated schools.

The Paradox of Reform in Black-Led Cities

The absence of an engaged public in local public school districts is a tragedy of American democracy. In *The Color of School Reform: Race, Politics, and the Challenge of Urban Education*, the authors examine the subject of civic capacity from a race perspective and provide an in-depth analysis of the political dynamics involving public schools in Baltimore, Detroit, and the District of Columbia. Each of these municipalities is heavily influenced by a Black-led political machine. Although during the time of the study, each city enjoyed levels of enthusiasm for school reform, each also had high dropout rates, poor performance on standardized tests, public discontent, and employer dissatisfaction with the skill levels of graduating students.[17]

The assumption of political power by African Americans in these three cities led to the widespread expectation that the transfer of power would result in better schools for children. However, the history of education reform in each of these cities reveals how any positive change has been extraordinarily difficult. In spite of numerous efforts during the late 1980s and the 1990s, evidence of substantial improvement in education was missing. On the contrary, school performance in each city declined, in some cases dramatically. Not only did reform efforts fail to provide significant improvement, but education authorities were also unable to generate substantial support for the sustained effort needed for broad-based education reform.[18]

The tendency to substitute small-scale initiatives for systemic reform is not unique to Black-led cities. However, the transition of political power to a Black-led power base seemed to predict an increased investment in schools that would address systemic social and economic inequalities. Yet, even when such investments were made in each of these

Black-led cities, there was an ongoing consensus that public schools were not meeting the public's vision for educating children.[18] This paradox leads us to explore the broader question of why, even in Black-led cities, education reform is so elusive.

Part Two

Mount Vernon, New York: Then and Now

Chapter 3

The Evolution of a Black-led City

The City of Mount Vernon, New York, owes its beginnings to the "back to the land movement," launched in 1850 by a group of New York residents who revolted against the rising cost of living in America's urban centers.[1] John Stevens, a New York City merchant in search of ways to escape the monopolization of land that was taking place in the New York metropolitan area, established the Home Industrial Association. Several hundred like-minded people of moderate means joined Stevens' organization and jointly purchased 250 acres of select land from the Town of Eastchester in October 1850. By 1852, a total of 300 homes had been built.

Similar to development of the early colonies, residents of Mount Vernon were quick to create a society that reflected a rich quality of life. In 1852, they established their first school in a temporary location on the second floor of an unfurnished house at Fifth Avenue and Third Street. A permanent structure was built the following year. In spite of its humble beginnings, Mount Vernon's early educational system became recognized as one of the better ones in the Empire State and, by 1917, a selling point to attract new residents to the area.

By the time the village was incorporated in 1853, settlements in other parts of the area were growing. East Mount Vernon, Central Mount Vernon, Fleetwood, and Chester Hill all became part of what constituted Mount Vernon proper. Its first civic organization—the Literary Club—was established in the 1850s, followed by the Horticultural Society and the Clinton Hook Fire Department. The first hospital was established in 1890.

Formation of a Black Community

The formation of a Black community in Mount Vernon during the late nineteenth century was a significant development in the course of Mount Vernon's history. Although a small number of free Blacks and former slaves were part of the early settlement, their role in the planning of this emerging village was circumscribed by their social standing at that time. By the late nineteenth century, however, Mount Vernon was one of the few areas with an inventory of multi-family dwellings. This housing stock was considered suitable housing for Blacks and immigrant laborers and offered an impetus for minority and immigrant groups to settle in the area. It was also fashionable for well-to-do White families in the city to employ Black help. Hiring domestic help was a sign of social distinction and served as a status symbol—an extension of the enduring legacy of slavery.

Mount Vernon received its first wave of Black residents in the nineteenth century as southern migrants and immigrants from the West Indies settled in the area. Although jobs were scarce, the number of Blacks continued to multiply. It was evident to many who arrived that life in the North, although difficult, was more humane than the horrors and intimidations that were taking place in the South. In the 1890s, there was little or no evidence of a Black middle class. Although some Blacks owned small businesses, the majority—almost 90 percent—worked as domestic servants, porters, seamstresses, and in other menial posts.

By 1890, there were 177 Blacks in Mount Vernon. By the start of World War I, there were 1,345. Most Blacks who migrated to Mount Vernon from the South came from Virginia, North Carolina, and South Carolina. Most were male, unmarried, unskilled, and the first generation born free from slavery. All were in search of the American dream. Wealthy southern Whites also migrated to Mount Vernon and the surrounding areas. Many of them brought their Black servants who often lived on the property of their employers until they eventually found places of their own in Mount Vernon. The Black population enrolled their children in the local public school district.

Grace Baptist Church, the Great Centennial African Methodist Episcopal Zion Church, and Macedonia Baptist Church were the leading religious institutions that shaped black society in the nineteenth century. Religious institutions served as a symbol of hope for many Black families and provided the community with leadership, traditional programs and services, and moral direction. Further, the Black church played a significant role in the life of the immigrant, serving as a beacon of hope for those who believed in God and the American dream. To combat racism and discrimination, Blacks and liberal Whites worked together to establish local branches of the National Association for the Advancement of Colored People and the National Urban League.

At the turn of the twentieth century, although leaders in America were predicting that the next hundred years would result in the fulfillment of America's promise of democracy, African Americans were not as optimistic. Segregation laws in the South and overt discrimination in the North were realities African Americans faced on a daily basis. African Americans living in Mount Vernon were not subjected to the life-threatening realities of the South, but even in this relatively congenial city, the condition of African Americans was precarious. Membership policies of labor unions excluded them from employment and limited their access to social mobility. More than any other group, Blacks spent most of their incomes on necessities. To make ends meet, women worked and families took lodgers into their homes to subsidize their incomes. Shut out of mainstream employment, African Americans established small family businesses, many of which operated out of their homes.

Geographical and Racial Segregation

The south side of Mount Vernon was unofficially designated as the black community in 1937. The defining moment came as a result of the construction of the New York to New Haven railroad system. The track for the railroad expansion went through the center of the city, with its physical presence creating a symbolic divide that forever changed the perception of the city as having distinctive north and south sides. The "other side" was synonymous with the "wrong side" of the city, the side for Blacks and the poor. Throughout urban America, sections reserved for Blacks often had names with racist connotations; for example, *Niggertown, Buzzard's Alley,* and *Bronzeville. Black Bottom* referred to the section reserved for Blacks in Mount Vernon, which extended from Second Street on the north to Sanford Boulevard on the south, and from South Fourth Avenue on the east to Thirteenth Avenue on the west. Incidentally, this neighborhood had been the home of the first settlers. It was passed down to Italians who migrated to the area at the turn of the nineteenth century to become the labor force needed to dig the split for the railroad expansion. They later settled in the southwest section, especially along South Seventh Avenue, near Third Street, in coldwater flats that were built in the 1890s to accommodate immigrant construction laborers working on the now-defunct New York, Westchester, and Boston Railway.

By 1935, an estimated 71 percent of the Black population lived in the Black Bottom section of Mount Vernon. This area became the most congested area of the city and among the most densely populated in the nation. A 1935 slum clearance survey sponsored by the Westchester Club revealed that housing for Blacks was deplorable, consisting of old buildings and rooming houses beyond profitable repair. Plumbing, heating, and ventilation were poor and private bathroom facilities were scarce luxuries. In spite of these conditions, rental fees were at a premium.

These conditions were the driving force behind the demand, initiated in 1939 by Rev. Benjamin Levister, for public housing. As Pastor of Grace Baptist Church and a leading community activist in the early 1930s, Reverend Levister had fought for the rights of Blacks in Mount Vernon, and singlehandedly fought the battle to integrate Mount Vernon's most famous restaurant—The Bee Hive—as well as Westchester County beaches. Outraged by the living conditions in the city, the pastor took the issue of slum housing to the city fathers. Although earlier attempts by the Westchester Women's Club and *The Daily Argus* to address the issue of poor housing had failed, he was determined to win the battle for decent housing for his people, using his own organization, the Mount Vernon Housing Advisory Council, to launch letter writing campaigns. He also joined forces with the Morris Link Post #1117 and the Westchester Committee Against Racial Discrimination. By 1940, Reverend Levister's coalition had expanded to 84 organizations in support of his slum clearance plan and the establishment of a local housing authority to carry out a plan for building low-income housing. In 1942, his dream was realized. Reverend Levister died in 1950, the very year Levister Towers, Mount Vernon's first public housing complex, was opened.

Emergence of the Black Middle Class

Even though the majority of the Black population was then poor and lived in Black Bottom, more prosperous, middle-class Blacks had moved west toward Mundy Lane and bought homes vacated by White families by the late 1920s. This area grew into a well-kept, integrated community. It remained so until the 1930s when signs of White flight began to emerge. Although this community became increasingly Black, it remained a well-kept, stable neighborhood. As more upwardly mobile Italians began to move into the north Bronx and the north side of Mount Vernon, Black homeownership and rentals increased and expanded, especially along Ninth and Tenth Avenues and Bushnell Place.

Racial discrimination impeded the expansion of the Black middle class into other sections of Mount Vernon. For example, it was virtually impossible for Blacks to purchase or rent homes on the north side. White homeowners who lived on all White streets were ostracized if they sold or rented their homes to Black families. Many homeowner associations went as far as organizing drives to insert restrictive covenants in their mortgages to prohibit the sale or rental of homes and apartments to Blacks.

In spite of these restrictions, the Black middle class continued to thrive within the confines of the southwest borders of Mount Vernon. Some of the best evidence of Black middle-class life in Mount Vernon during the 1930s and 1940s is found in advertisements of the annual dances of their social clubs. In 1935, there were at least twenty-five social clubs, many of which had begun before 1920. Among them were the Twilight Girls, the Jolly Boys, Les Petites Femmes, Buddy-Q's Girls Club, Alpha Deity Club, Lone Star, Lucky 13's, South Side Social Club, and the Silent Aces. There were class distinctions among the various clubs, and when new families and individuals moved into the community, their recruitment into a particular club depended on their social standing.

During the 1960s, Mount Vernon experienced major shifts in its racial composition and a significant expansion of the Black middle class. Between 1960 and 1965, the city realized a loss of 7,919 Whites and a gain of 4,282 Blacks. This gain in the Black population did not offset the emigration of Whites and, as a result, by 1965, the city had realized a net decline in its population. There was a 152 percent increase in the Black population between 1950 and 1965. During the same period, the White population declined by 17 percent. The key to understanding how the Black community evolved and grew in such proportions was the loss of 14,084 Whites from the south side of town. White flight in Mount Vernon did not result in a mass exodus from the city; rather, it was more a relocation of Whites from the south side to the north side. As Whites moved to the north side of town, they freed up a large housing stock, especially in Vernon Heights and Chester Heights—communities well known for their large, nineteenth century single-family homes. With this new availability of middle-class housing stock, Mount Vernon became a haven for middle-class Black urban families seeking affordable housing in the suburbs.

Unlike the earlier wave of poor, rural Black migrants, this new wave of Black residents included urbanites with professional skills and middle-class aspirations who took advantage of the White flight that was occurring and proudly purchased homes along tree-lined streets on the south side of the city. Many celebrities moved to Mount Vernon in the 1950s and late 1960s, including Dr. George Edmund Haynes, co-founder of the National Urban League; Congressman Adam Clayton Powell and his wife, Hazel Scott; famed jazz pianists; Al Jaj Malik Shabazz, also know as Malcolm X, and his wife Dr. Betty Shabazz; former prime minister of Uganda, Godfrey Binais; the parents of Broadway actress Stephanie Mills; vocalist and pianist, Nina Simone; and actors Ossie Davis, Ruby Dee, and Sidney Poitier—to name a few.

Growing Prominence of Black Politicians

The period between 1955 and 1965 was a crucial decade for the African American community. Jim Crow was no longer legal, and the future for African Americans was dynamic and full of hope. The Reverend Dr. Martin Luther King, Jr. and the Civil Rights Movement spawned new, young leadership in Black communities throughout the country, including the City of Mount Vernon. Black churches on the south side continued to grow in prominence by taking bold steps to fight social and economic inequality. This was a period when many Blacks first broke through institutional racial barriers that had prevailed for centuries, and Mount Vernon's Black community produced many examples. After ten unsuccessful attempts between 1931 and 1952, the first Black was appointed to the Mount Vernon School Board in 1953, and elected to a full term the following year. In 1955, Edward Williams became the first Black male teacher in Mount Vernon, and plans for a new high school promised integration at the secondary level. The first Black fireman had been hired in 1952, and the first Black was elected during the same year to the Westchester Board of Supervisors. In 1953, Alfred Brandon was appointed Mount Vernon's first police sergeant, and in 1956, Harold Hamilton became the first Black corporation counsel and prosecutor.

A Focal Point for Civil Rights

With the rise of the nonviolent Civil Rights Movement between 1956 and 1968, the City of Mount Vernon was at the forefront of political action in Westchester County, with its Black churches playing a significant role in its leadership. In response to the call to support the Montgomery bus boycott that began in December 1955, more than 600 Mount Vernon citizens pledged their moral and financial support to Blacks fighting discrimination in the South. On February 27, 1956, a rally was held at the Greater Centennial AME Zion Church, which encouraged a great deal of interracial and ecumenical support for the boycott. Mayor Joseph P. Vaccarella, Reverend E. Leslie Wood, who was President of the Mount Vernon Council of Churches, Reverend Robert G. Davis of Vernon Heights Congregational Church, Rabbi Max Maccoby of the Free Synagogue of Westchester, Rabbi Joseph H. Wise of the Jewish Center, and John J. Yannantuono, a member of the Board of Education, comprised this multi-racial and ecumenical effort. Reverend Richard H. Dixon, Jr., pastor of the Macedonia Baptist Church went on to chair the Westchester Christian Leadership Conference, a newly established local affiliate of the national movement. He coordinated several successful events that increased visibility and raised public awareness of the plight of African Americans and their fight for social justice, nationally and locally.

The Civil Rights Movement was also an impetus for change in Mount Vernon. Many Blacks who had migrated to Mount Vernon were familiar with the injustices that took place in the South. As a result, they welcomed having an active role in the call for civic action. More than 400 Mount Vernon residents participated in the August 28, 1963 March on Washington and were present to hear the Reverend Dr. Martin Luther King Jr.'s famous "I Have a Dream" speech.

A New Battleground for Equality

Similar to the way in which demands for public housing had become a battleground during the 1930s, public schools in Mount Vernon became the new battleground where the fight for equality was fought for more than three decades. In the nineteenth century, Black children received the rudiments of education in neighborhood schools. Through the end of that century, they remained a very small minority within the district. During the first twenty-five years of the twentieth century, however, the enrollment of Black students increased significantly, especially on the south side of the city. Racially segregated housing patterns resulted in inequitably segregated neighborhood schools. Schools on the south side serving the Black community were not as well-equipped as schools on the north side that served exclusively White communities.

The fight for equality in the school district began in 1964, with African Americans and White liberals working together to attack de facto segregation in the city. This fight led to a mass exodus of White families who feared the changing demographics of the city and saw it as a threat to their neighborhoods and the school district. By 1969, the proportion of White students was declining; and by 1972, only three schools within the district had a majority of White students. In spite of the increase in African American students, the policymaking school board was comprised of members of the White community and remained solidly under the political influence of the powerful Italian Civic Association (ICA). The Board of Education did all it could to fight integration. It resisted affirmative-action goals and timetables and was even unwilling to commit to the principles of integration.

The school district's budget was far greater than the city's budget and was the major economic engine for the city. The school district was the largest employer in the city. Having political control over the school board provided the ICA with a stronghold over a large proportion of the resources within the district. It wielded great influence over jobs and lucrative contracts to vendors for products and services. Having such influence over the Board of Education enabled the ICA to control every apparatus leading to social mobility in the city. Unwilling to relinquish its stronghold, the ICA fought vigorously, not only against integration, but also to maintain its influence over the city's economic engine by ensuring that only candidates backed by their organization were elected to the Board of Education.

School board elections became the forum for racial rhetoric with inflammatory remarks and actions coming from both the Black and White communities. Elections took on a negative racial tone to frighten the community into action. Members of the Black community took part in church-led sit-ins, prayer vigils, and protest demonstrations. The fears of the White community centered on the increasing Black majority and its potential to take over the Board of Education. Such an outcome would likely bring loss of White control over the district's economic and political apparatus.

Racial tension became even worse when, in 1973, the U.S. Department of Health, Education and Welfare ruled that Mount Vernon practiced segregation in the hiring of teachers. The fight for integration polarized the community, resulting in great tension between Black and White groups. Wounds and hard feelings from the racial conflict remained unhealed through the 1970s and beyond. The possibility of the Black community's controlling jobs, political patronage, and lucrative contracts was becoming too much of a reality for those who benefited from a White-controlled political machine. At the same time, the political influence of the ICA made the goal of attaining control of the Board of Education a difficult one to reach.

Under the political influence of the ICA, the school board election and governance processes did not encourage full public participation. Any attempt to educate the public was sabotaged by emotionalism and charges of radicalism and racism. This practice made all minority candidates submit to a well-oiled political machine. The Jewish community was also besieged by the political struggle for control. Committed to quality education as well as supporting the plight of disadvantaged groups, the Jewish community became caught up in the political fight between the African American and White communities. It became increasingly difficult for the Jewish community to win school board seats without the support of the ICA. Gaining this support often came at the cost of political concessions that were not always in the best interest of the at-large community. This practice ultimately caused friction within the ICA as well as with Jewish school board candidates who sought endorsement. This eventually led to the weakening of ICA dominance.

Transition to a Black Political Power Base

Sparked by the Civil Rights Movement, residents within the Black community recognized the potential of their political strength and began to organize in ways that maximized the political impact of their growing population. During the 1960s, many existing and emerging groups in the Black community focused their attention on voter registration and building a new political machine comprised of Blacks and liberal Whites. Similar to what was taking place throughout the country, Mount Vernon experienced its share of political action, race riots, and conflict within its own Black community.

The religious community played an important role in shaping the political environment and encouraging the non-violence that characterized the Civil Rights Era. The church also played a leading role in fostering the transition to a Black political power base. In 1967, Dr. Samuel Austin, Sr., Pastor of Grace Baptist Church, became the first African American to seek election to the office of mayor. Although his bid was unsuccessful, a Black political power base was emerging and groundwork was being laid for an inevitable political takeover.

Less than two decades later, two major political victories were won. First, three Black candidates won school board seats in 1984, defeating candidates who were backed by the ICA. This came as a result of a split within the ICA and its loss of support from the Jewish community. Their election, in essence, broke the political stranglehold of the once-powerful ICA. Second, Black and White voters came together in 1985 to elect Mount Vernon's first Black mayor, the Honorable Ronald Blackwood, breaking the strong political control of the Republican Party. These two events resulted in the Black community no longer identified as being owned by either the Democratic Party or the Republican Party.

The New Black Political Regime

Although the Black community experienced a major victory, mistakes were made and many people, Black and White, were hurt in the political process. In 1999, after a thirty-year effort, the African American community gained majority representation on the district's Board of Education, ushering in the new Black political regime. This transition to Black leadership has continued into the twenty-first century. Blacks continue to fill local governmental posts, including the office of the mayor, important commissionerships and judgeships, and a majority of seats on the city council. This new Black leadership has also used its influence to get out the vote to elect government officials at county and state levels and—more importantly—to maintain Black majority representation on the Mount Vernon Board of Education.

In the course of this transition, the once powerful ICA was displaced by the United Black Clergy (UBC), which, in turn, was perceived by the public as a large component of the new Black political machine. The church continues to play a significant role in education politics, as reflected in the number of church trustees endorsed by members of the clergy who have then won their campaigns for election.

In spite of this transfer of power, Mount Vernon—once touted as the most prominent community in Westchester County—entered the twenty-first century as the poorest municipality in the county. As in many urban, Black-led cities, the transfer of power did not change the socioeconomic conditions of the people who stood to gain the most—African Americans and other disenfranchised groups.

Chapter 4

The Mount Vernon School District in 2007

Westchester County, New York, located north of New York City, in close proximity to the metropolitan areas of New York, New Jersey, and Connecticut, features natural topography and magnificent waterways and that make it one of the most desirable suburban locations in the region. It is home to the headquarters or major sites of ten Fortune 500 companies whose combined value is estimated to be $200 billion. In addition, an estimated 131,150 businesses located in the county generate $9 billion in sales annually. These companies and businesses make Westchester County the fourth highest generator of revenues in the New York metropolitan area, giving the county one of the highest median per capita personal incomes in the region. The county enjoys a reputation for having some of the best schools in the country and a rich housing stock that is spread across an array of hamlets, towns, villages, and cities. Residents also enjoy a wealth of health and human service agencies.[1]

Located in the southern tier of Westchester County is the city of Mount Vernon. As shown in Figure 4.1, it is among six urban centers in the county. During the nineteenth and twentieth centuries, Mount Vernon served as a magnet for middle-class families in search of a fine suburban quality of life. Being situated close to New York City, with a stock of nineteenth century homes and a reputation for quality schools, Mount Vernon was then among the most sought-after communities in the State of New York. Today, Mount Vernon is distinguished as the first Black-led municipality in the State of New York.[2]

Figure 4.1
Map of Westchester County, NY

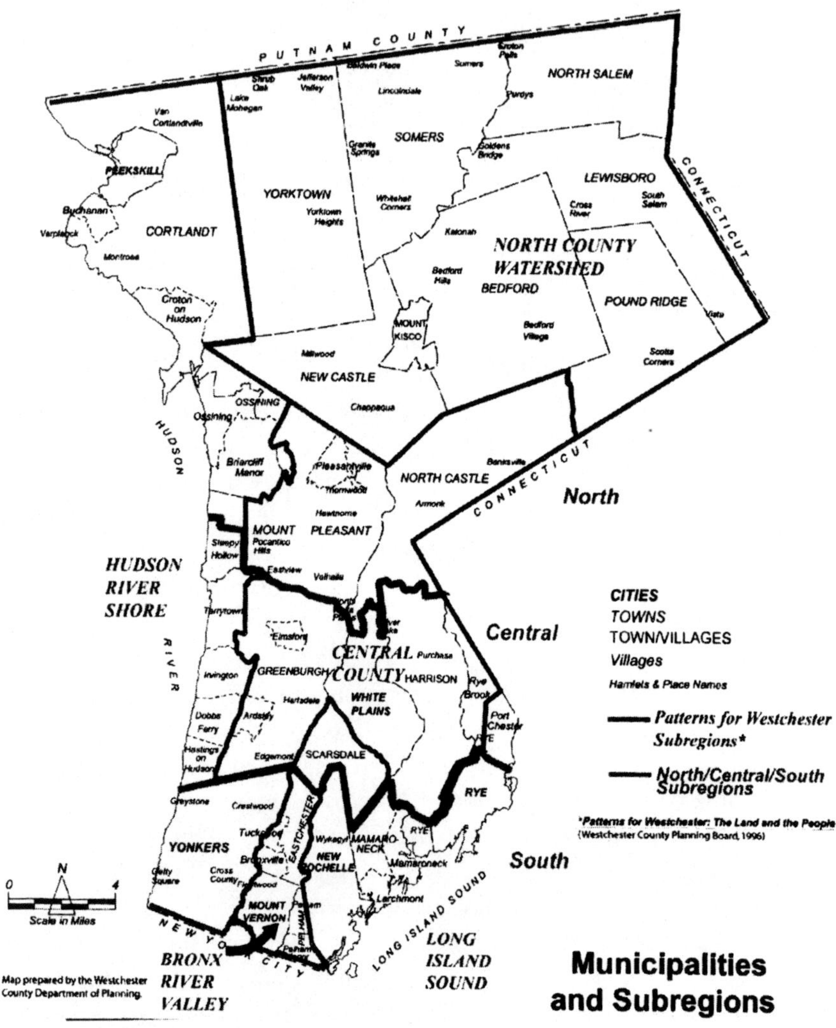

A City in Distress

After more than two centuries of prominence, Mount Vernon has emerged in the twenty-first century as the poorest community in the county. With a population of 68,381 residing in an area of 4.4 square miles, Mount Vernon is the most densely populated municipality in Westchester County and has the highest concentration of minority groups.[3] In 2000, its poverty rate was 13 percent and adults over age 25 who had achieved a bachelor's degree or higher comprised only 26 percent of its population.[4] As shown in Table 4.1, Mount Vernon reported a median household income of $41,128 in 2000, which was the lowest among the five cities that reported median incomes below the county's median of $63,582.

Table 4.1
Median Incomes Below Westchester Countywide Levels for 1999

City	Median Household Income
Mount Vernon	$41,128
Yonkers	$44,633
Peekskill	$47,177
New Rochelle	$55,513
White Plains	$58,545

Note. County 1999 Median Household Income for Westchester County was $63,582. From Westchester County Department of Planning, *Databook Westchester County, New York.* 2010.

According to a 2004–2005 needs assessment conducted by the Westchester County Department of Social Services and the Westchester County Youth Bureau, the Mount Vernon School District (MVSD) is identified as having families and children in need of supplemental services.[5] In the 2006–2007 school year, the total kindergarten-through-grade-12 student enrollment was 9,735. Its student population was 80 percent African American; 13 percent Latino; 6 percent White; and 1 percent American Indian, Alaskan, Asian, or Pacific Islander. Forty-six percent of students were eligible for free or reduced-price lunches, and 8 percent of students had limited English proficiency.[6]

In spite of the county's reputation for having a large number of well-funded public school districts that produce high-achieving students, Mount Vernon High School ranks as Westchester County's lowest performing school.[7] Although significant progress had been made in student performance at the elementary school level, Mount Vernon's high school graduation rate of 59.7 percent in 2006–2007 was the lowest in Westchester County.[8]

Student Performance in the Mount Vernon School District

With regard to student performance at the elementary school level, the MVSD reported that a majority of students in each of its elementary schools scored at or above Level 3 (Proficiency) of the state learning standards in English Language Arts (ELA) and mathematics during the 2006–2007 school year. Overall student performance at elementary schools in the district was competitive with overall New York State results, as shown in Table 4.2.

Table 4.2
English Language Arts and Mathematics Assessments in Grades 3–5: Percentage of Students Scoring at Level 3 or 4

	English Language Arts		Mathematics	
Grade Level	Mount Vernon SD	New York State	Mount Vernon SD	New York State
3	71 %	67 %	86 %	85 %
4	77 %	68 %	84 %	80 %
5	72 %	68 %	71 %	76 %

From *New York State District Report Card: Accountability and Overview Report 2006-2007- Mount Vernon City School District.* (New York State Department of Education, 2008), 17-23.

Student performance, measured by state learning standards at the middle school grade levels, was less successful. As shown in Table 4.3, overall student performance indicating proficiency in both ELA and mathematics was below overall New York State results in all three grades during the 2006–2007 school year. Two middle schools were cited as needing remedial action: Longfellow Middle School was classified as *In need of Improvement* for a second consecutive year, and A. B. Davis Middle School was classified as *Under Corrective Action*.

Table 4.3
English Language Arts and Mathematics Assessments in Grades 6–8: Percentage of Students Scoring at Level 3 or 4

	English Language Arts		**Mathematics**	
Grade Level	Mount Vernon SD	New York State	Mount Vernon SD	New York State
6	60 %	63 %	65 %	71 %
7	38 %	58 %	35 %	67 %
8	40 %	57 %	29 %	59 %

From *New York State District Report Card: Accountability and Overview Report 2006-2007- Mount Vernon City School District.* (New York State Department of Education, 2008), 24-29.

The MVSD is among seven districts within the county cited as needing continuous support for ancillary educational services: Mount Vernon, Tarrytown, Peekskill, Port Chester, Yonkers, Ossining, and New Rochelle. Each of these districts has a high concentration of minority students that are not performing on state assessments at or above the state standard of proficiency. The percentage of students achieving scores at or above the state reference point in elementary ELA improved significantly between 1999 and 2003 in all target area schools. However, scores for the MVSD were the lowest among the seven in-need districts.

As shown in Table 4.4, incremental increases for Mount Vernon students are apparent in the percentage of fourth-grade students scoring at or above the state reference point in the areas of ELA and mathematics. However, comparatively little or no progress in ELA occurred over the same period for eighth-grade students. For example, the percentage of eighth-grade students who achieved proficiency in mathematics by the 2002–2003 school year increased. However, even at its apex over this five-year period, (1999 and 2003) over 50 percent of eighth-grade students continued to fall below the level of proficiency in mathematics. This level of achievement was the third lowest among the seven districts.[9]

Table 4.4

Trends in Students Scoring At or Above State Reference Point (SRP) in English Language Arts (ELA) and Mathematics (Math) Assessments in Grades 4 and 8

	School Year				
Assessment	1998–1999	1999–2000	2000–2001	2001–2002	2002–2003
ELA 4	36 %	48 %	74 %	78 %	83 %
Math 4	51 %	60 %	79 %	79 %	86 %
ELA 8	24 %	19 %	19 %	26 %	23 %
Math 8	14 %	16 %	12 %	35 %	38 %

From *2000-2004 Needs Assessment: Supplement to the Child and Family Service Plan*. (Westchester County Department of Social Service and Westchester County Youth Bureau), 27.

With regard to student performance among high school students, scores on secondary level math and English tests after four years of instruction improved in the 2002 and 2003 cohorts. Yet, as shown in Table 4.5, the percentage of Mount Vernon high school students who scored at or above the state standard on state exams was below the overall results for New York State students for both cohorts. A total 683 students entered the 2003 cohort. By 2007, 202 students had dropped out of school and only 390 graduated.[10]

In addition to these measurements of student performance and findings of need, there were other signs that the MVSD was in distress. School-community relations in Mount Vernon were at their worst in 2007, with recent indicators suggesting a community-wide no-vote of confidence for its public school district. An estimated 25 to 30 percent of students who graduated from Mount Vernon's sixth grade did not enroll in any of the district's middle schools, as parents choose alternative educational settings for their children. Consequently, parent participation, along with student performance, particularly at the middle and high school grades, was low. Less than six percent of registered voters participated in school board elections, and school board meetings were mired in discussions aimed at fixing blame for a failed public school system. In 2008, the community was so dissatisfied, a referendum on the school budget was voted down on two occasions, forcing the district to operate under an austerity budget.

Table 4.5

District's Total Cohort Results of Students Scoring at Level 3 or 4 in Secondary-Level English and Math after Four Years of Instruction

	Secondary Level English Exam		**Secondary Level Mathematics Exam**	
Cohort	Mount Vernon SD	New York State	Mount Vernon SD	New York State
2003	55 %	73 %	59 %	74 %
2002	51 %	69 %	58 %	71 %

From *New York State School Report Card: Accountability and Overview Report 2006-2007* – Mount Vernon School District (New York State Department of Education, 2008), 31-32.

Part Three

Voices from the Mount Vernon School District

Chapter 5

Respondents and Stakeholders

Mount Vernon's population is diverse, with people of more than 98 nationalities living within its 4.4 square-mile radius. Within the Black or African American community, one finds African Americans born in the United States, Caribbean Americans from islands of the West Indies, and first- or second-generation immigrants from the African continent, many of whom maintain a distinct identity. Similarly, a range of ethnicities are found within the Latino community, including Brazilians, Puerto Ricans, Dominicans, and Mexicans. The White population includes Anglo-Saxons, Jews, Italians, Portuguese, and other groups of European descent. To respect the rich diversity that exists within these communities, people from the many cultures that make up the Black or African American community are referred to here as People of African Descent (POAD). People whose origins were in Latin American countries are described as people of Latino Descent; and Caucasians or Whites are referred to as people of European Descent.

Interview Respondents

Drawing from Mount Vernon's diverse population, 78 respondents were selected for in-depth interviews. When compared with the 2000 Census profile for Mount Vernon, this group of respondents was representative of the city's diverse population: 63 percent were of African descent; 25 percent were of European descent; and 5 percent were of Latino descent. The sample was almost evenly divided by gender: 51 percent of respondents were male, and 49 percent were female. Among the respondents who indicated their marital status, 67 percent were married, 19 percent were single, 9 percent were divorced, and 5 percent were widowed.

The majority of respondents (91 percent) were products of the public school system. Their levels of educational attainment were much higher than those of the general population of Mount Vernon: 21 percent of respondents reported having a four-year college degree compared with 14 percent of Mount Vernon residents; and 21 percent of respondents reported having a graduate or professional degree compared with 10 percent of Mount Vernon residents.

Among those respondents who reported having children, approximately 80 percent sent their children to public schools. However, only 42 percent of Mount Vernon respondents with children indicated that their children attended public schools within the MVSD.

Stakeholder Groups

To capture views from a range of relevant perspectives, the sample population comprised representatives from four stakeholder groups. One was education specialists (Specialists), which included educators, administrators, and persons especially knowledgeable about school systems. Specialists constituted 29 percent of the sample. Stakeholders from other community-based organizations (CBOs) included individuals who represented children's advocacy groups, neighborhood organizations, religious organizations, and PTAs. CBO stakeholders constituted 30 percent of the sample. Stakeholders from communities at large (CALs) included individuals who lived in the community, but were not necessarily affiliated with any organization and who might, therefore, have been underrepresented. CAL stakeholders constituted 25 percent of the sample. Members of the fourth group were generally influential stakeholders (Influentials), individuals whose position or status made them potentially important actors in matters related to education policy. Influentials constituted 17 percent of the sample.

Ten respondents (13 percent) belonged to more than one stakeholder group. In some instances, a respondent's secondary voice was so strong that it seemed important enough to distinguish his or her primary and secondary responses. In those instances, respondents were assigned a secondary stakeholder classification, as shown in Table 5.1.

Table 5.1
Respondents with Influence in More Than One Stakeholder Group

	Secondary Stakeholder Group				
Primary Stakeholder Group	Specialists	CBO	CAL	Influentials	Total
Specialists	0	0	3	0	3
CBO	2	0	1	0	3
CAL	1	2	0	0	3
Influentials	1	0	0	0	1
Total	4	2	4	0	10

In many instances, their dual perspectives provided some of the most valuable insights into the complexities of the public and its relationship with the school district. For example, there were several Specialists who spoke with expertise about the educational system, while also providing insight regarding their frustrations as parents or community members, or both.

Chapter 6

The Public's Commitment to Public Education

The majority (91 percent) of respondents were products of public education, 80 percent of whom had chosen to enroll their own children in public schools. Whether they attended segregated public schools in the South or de facto segregated schools in the North during the 1960s integration movement, or, as immigrants, discovered the gift of free education after travelling to America, many recall fond memories of their public school experience and the important role it played in shaping their lives. Almost all respondents describe the high educational standards to which they were held as children. Although many respondents grew up under poor and often inequitable conditions, most expressed how education was the cornerstone of their community and at the core of their family values. The following is from a local resident who grew up on Mount Vernon's south side.

> My mother had, I have her high school diploma. I had it framed. And she graduated from Plymouth Colored High School. . . . And when she came here in 1950 with a Jim Crow education and demanded that each of her children understand the importance of education, she said, "It will be the road out of poverty for all of us." And she was absolutely correct. So from the housing authority, she educated five children. All of them have matriculated in the highest citadels of learning—the highest PhDs, master's degrees, all of them. And she never got anything more than a Jim Crow education. So even here at our church, it's one of the biggest things that I jump up and down and scream about. We fill out applications, we call, we do everything that

we gotta do. Everybody must go. If you go and fail, you gotta go. Go fail over there. Good place to fail. That's the way we look at it.

Another resident from the Brazilian community uses the following illustration to describe how important education was in his family. He recalls a conversation he had with the boyfriend of his teenage daughter:

When he finished high school, "I've got to take some time off." One year. And last year, last November, I say, "You like [my daughter]?" "Oh, I love your daughter." "You really love my daughter?" "I do." "But she's in college." "Oh, that's all right. I want to become a cop." "Oh, great, when can it happen?" "Oh, next year." Which is 2007. I say, "Let me tell you something. If you become a cop, you just have a high school diploma. You don't have a college diploma. You're not going to graduate from college? You're going to be just a cop? You're not going to be a sergeant or captain or lieutenant?" "I'll go back to college, after I'm in the department." I said, "No, you won't! Now, I'm going to give you two options: Number one, register yourself at the next college season, which is going to be January. I don't care which college. I don't care how many hours you're going to put in. I want you in college next year, 2007. Option number two, you see the front door to the house? Leave the house." "What? You can't." "I can. You listen to me or you take my daughter and you move out. She's nineteen. She's grown up enough that you can take care of her, take her with you, and she gonna be a college graduate and you're going to be just a high school diploma kid." He said, "You're not serious." I said, "I'm serious as I can think. Option number one, get yourself back to college." So he took option number one. "I don't care if you break up with my daughter next year—I don't care. You don't have to marry my daughter. But I want you back in college. You allowed coming back to my house in 2007." So I asked him after this, "What do you need?" "Oh, I don't have a computer." So I said, "Okay," and at Christmas I bought him a computer, a Dell computer. I said, "Where's your registration?" He said, "Here's my registration." So, he's in college.

The immigrants who participated in the study had a zeal for education. In spite of how much they struggled to make ends meet, education remained important to them. The notion of free education was too phenomenal for them to pass up. For example, the daughter of an African family who participated in the study was a graduate of Mount Vernon

High School. She was attending a local junior college and had little patience for those students who were not interested in obtaining an education.

The majority of the respondents interviewed believed that Mount Vernon residents valued the institution of public education as well. When asked how the public ranked the institution of public education on a scale from 1 to 10, with 1 being of the utmost importance and 10 being irrelevant, 36% of respondents felt the public would rank public schools either as a one or two (see Table 6.1).

Table 6.1
Mount Vernon Public Respondents' Judgment of Importance of Public Education

	Stakeholder Group				
Rank	**Specialist**	**CBO**	**CAL**	**Influentials**	**Total**
1-2 Very Important	8 %	12 %	10 %	5 %	35 %
3-4 Important	8 %	12 %	3 %	5 %	28 %
5-6 Somewhat Important	6 %	4 %	7 %	4 %	21 %
7-8 Not Very Important	5 %	3 %	4 %	1 %	13 %
9-10 Irrelevant	0 %	0 %	3 %	0 %	3 %
Total	27 %	31 %	27 %	15 %	100 %

Respondents were asked to reconcile their responses with the fact that only 1,600 people voted in the last school board election—an estimated 6% of all registered voters. Many respondents spoke about the apathy that existed among parents and other residents. They attributed this apathy to dissatisfaction with the state of education in Mount Vernon, and the sense that nothing could be done to improve conditions. The following quote is from an elected official:

> I think that that's just a disgrace, to think that 1,200 [sic] people are deciding the fate of an entire school district, an entire institution with all the implications of that. That's a very scary thing. I think Mount Vernon has about 80,000 people living in it. And I think that there are about 30,000 registered voters, and for only 1,200 people to vote for the school district, I just thinks shows the—I don't want to say apathy—but just the dissatisfaction. I think that that's more a reflection of,

> not disinterest, but dissatisfaction, since it doesn't matter what you do, things aren't going to get any better.

Some respondents raised the fact that many adults in Mount Vernon are former students who were educated by a failed public school system and now lack the skills or sophistication to understand the importance of education. Having been failed by the system, many residents no longer value education as the cornerstone of their family values. One respondent spoke about the effects of an undereducated population:

> Mount Vernon is a diverse community. I think that's a strength. Even the African American population is extremely diverse. I think that's a strength. I think that bodes good for education. . . . I think that there is a general appreciation among the people—it may not show up in the voting—for public education. I think people in this community value it. I would say overwhelmingly, most of the people in Mount Vernon are products of public education. That's good and bad. The bad side of that is that some of the inadequacies of the school system have been perpetuated into multi-generations. So we end up having parents who are undereducated and those parents are intimidated by the system, so they don't know how to advocate on behalf of the children. So it's a terrible cycle of when you mis-educate.

The findings suggest that there may be truth in this perception. Respondents from across all stakeholder groups spoke of this phenomenon. However, there were respondents with whom we spoke who believed they had been failed by the public schools. Contrary to public perceptions, there were some who were actively involved in their local school, working to ensure their children would have a different experience. One young parent described herself as having been a teenage mom who gave birth when she was 14 years old. She returned to school after her child was born with an approved plan to complete her middle-school requirements and go on to high school. Although she was excited about returning to school, the combination of factors, including medical complications with her newborn, a bureaucratic mix-up, and a breakdown in communications, resulted in her quitting school and pursuing her GED on her own. The following quote provides insight into this parent's thinking and the active role she plays in her child's education:

> They do have that teacher-to-parent thing that's going on, where parents feel like it's the teacher's job to educate their kids and their job to

> discipline them. But nothing is going back and forth and then the teachers don't want to call home anymore, when they should call. 'Cause [teachers] don't want to deal with the ignorant parents, whose children "never do anything wrong." It's like this problem is not on one side. If there's a disagreement, you can never look at anything and say that it's on one side. You have to find the fault in both sides, you know? But with [name of daughter] last year they're calling me to tell me that she's failing at the end of the marking period. And I'm like, "Well, where were you the first ten weeks in the marking period? I'm at the school. The kids know me. The teachers know me. Why didn't you call me?" Granted, I didn't get it done. Maybe if I'd have known it wasn't handed in or asked for. But at the same time, I'm a single parent. I work two jobs and I go to school. . . . Like, I need the extra help. So if [name of daughter] is not on point. Yes, it may become annoying for the teacher. But we in this together!

This young mother goes on to describe her relationship with the school and the difficulty she has in getting the service she believes her daughter needs.

> They know me because I go up there and fight. I go up there because they went and told me that [my daughter] has disabilities. She has ADD. And they want to tell me that she need to be on medication. And she can't be on medication. So now y'all still have to, by state law, educate her. And y'all need to put the programs in place to educate her whether she is scoring high average or not. 'Cause Mt. Vernon's disposition is that because [my daughter] is passing, they don't need to do anything. Well, my disposition is she should be doing better than she is if you would just put the support there to help her. In 6th grade I had a A/B student. Now that she's an F, can I get some help, please?

Another parent, who described her public school experience as not very helpful, discussed her battle to see her son through graduation. She spoke of the transition he had made from elementary to middle school, and how she was losing him to peer pressure. She acknowledges her son as having behavior problems and describes her fight and her frustration with school administrators to ensure her son gets the services he needs.

> He's now considered classified Special Ed. And you would think that, because I am a very vocal parent, and I'm always involved, that they would make sure they would break their back to accommodate my son. My son was missing assignments. I would have to go to the school

> and make sure that they give me the assignments. Then they would tell him if he didn't hand in an assignment, "Oh, well, he can't hand the assignment in now because it's too late." I said, "But—he has a 504 plan, so therefore he can hand in these assignments and, he will be able to and you need to change his grade." They refused. I had to go; I had to fight! As long as you're talking and you're yelling, then they will accommodate you. But when you're not—they just let these children fall in between the cracks. So my son has fallen in between the cracks, and he's a failing student. And he's not going down the right path and—I'm very concerned.

Although there are some parents who fit the description of a disenfranchised population, among them are parents who are actively involved with their children's education. In spite of their own experiences, they value the institution of public education and are very involved in their children's education. They were searching, with little success, for meaningful partnerships with the district based on mutual respect.

Many respondents spoke of Mount Vernon's being a bedroom community to a large segment of its population. The city's close proximity to New York City and its stock of beautiful homes attract people to Mount Vernon. Several respondents observed that many families from Mount Vernon's middle class do not value public education in Mount Vernon, but moved into the area with the intention of enjoying amenities of the nearby city, while sending their children to private schools. These families were more concerned with safety issues—controlling gang violence and maintaining low taxes. Some spoke of parents who send their children to elementary schools on the north side, but intend to leave once their children are old enough to enter middle school. Any involvement among these families was limited to their community school.

Chapter 7

A Shared Vision for Public Schools

The people of Mount Vernon had a clear sense of the type of school district they wanted for their children. An estimated 29 percent of all respondents cited a school culture conducive to learning as the most important element of their ideal school. An ideal school would have a culture of mutual respect among teachers, students, and parents, all working together toward a mutual goal. The second element most frequently identified for an ideal school was a dedicated and highly qualified staff, cited by 18 percent of all respondents. These respondents spoke of their ideal school as being staffed by teachers truly dedicated to the profession. They wanted teachers who would value the importance of learning outside of the classroom and helping children link learning to the world in which they live. They would be teachers who understood the importance of teaching moral values to children, values that reinforce a commitment to humanity. Respondents were interested in teachers who were committed to spending time after school and who were open to parents who want to be actively engaged in their children's learning experience.

Respondents were also interested in having building leaders who effectively support teachers, leaders to whom teachers can look up and to whom they can go with their problems. Respondents envisioned building leaders who would protect educators from the political environment in which they often find themselves operating. They should also be committed to the kind of teacher development that inspires teachers to reach their full educational potential. They wanted administrators who appreciate new teaching techniques and technologies and are committed to making them available to the teaching staff. Finally, there were many respondents who spoke about the need for a multi-racial teaching staff that is also multi-faceted in their interests in and approaches to learning. Members of this diverse faculty should both respect each other and be passionate about their work.

The third most frequently identified element for an ideal school was the need for a safe and orderly environment in which to learn and teach. This element was cited by 13.9 percent of all respondents who answered the question. There was no doubt in the minds of many respondents about the great importance of an orderly, safe school environment. It was described by many as the fundamental component that allows for good education. Two students who participated in an interview spoke with excitement about their ideal school. One had just graduated from the high school. The other had completed four years of college, and planned to return to the Mount Vernon district to teach. As they spoke about their ideal school, it became apparent that safety was an important element:

> I would try to find the best teachers for each category like English, math, and, computers. I love technology so we have computers and then when students need to do their work on the computer, there's enough computers for everybody to use them; and it would be a big school, like a university. So big you can't even find your room, you need help . . . and then get security guards, but good ones that have good references so if a student actually needs help, they could go to them, and they wouldn't be scared to actually be. . . . [You want to be sure that] the children are safe and [in] a good environment.

> Basically I want the school to have something that appeals to your child. Once they have something that's appealing to them, they're going to be willing to learn, but also the most essential is their safety. They should always feel safe, that's gonna be an environment where the safety's not a risk and once they know their safety's not secure, they're always gonna be in fear and intimidated and they're not gonna open their minds to learn.

Parents must feel absolutely confident that they are sending their children to a safe and orderly place of learning. Respondents pointed out that a safe setting needs to be created in the schools as well as throughout the community, so children can travel to and from school freely and comfortably. A state-of-the-art physical plant was also cited as a key element, equal to safety and order, comprising 13 percent of responses. This element was followed by a desire for smaller learning communities and strong parent and community participation (see Table 7.1).

Table 7.1
Respondents' Rankings for Key Elements of Ideal School

	Stakeholder Group				
Key Elements	**Specialist**	**CBO**	**CAL**	**Influentials**	**Total**
Physical Plant	4 %	6 %	4 %	0 %	14 %
Qualified Faculty/Staff	8 %	4 %	6 %	1 %	19 %
Safety/Social Order	7 %	4 %	3 %	1 %	15 %
Students Ready to Learn	1 %	1 %	0 %	1 %	3 %
Parent & Community Involvement	0 %	6 %	0 %	0 %	6 %
Culture of Learning	8 %	4 %	7 %	10 %	29 %
Smaller Learning Communities	0 %	4 %	1 %	3 %	8 %
Other	1 %	1 %	4 %	0 %	6 %
Total	29 %	30 %	25 %	16 %	100 %

Respondents had a clear sense of what was needed to build their ideal school. They talked about an important role for business. More than 40 percent of respondents who answered a question about businesses' having a role in education believed that businesses could provide financial and in-kind support. They could fund programs for extracurricular activities, such as sports and other programs that enable educators to expose students to learning outside of the classroom. Respondents talked about the need for after-school programs, where students can study and be safe while their parents are at work. Internship opportunities were cited by 33 percent of the respondents, noting the value inherent in introducing students to the world of work. In this role, business leaders could demonstrate the opportunities open to those who do well in school.

Less than 5 percent of respondents believed business should play a role in shaping education policy. There were some, however, who believed that business should play a role in policies that directly impact their operations. For example, many respondents spoke of a problem between merchants on Gramatan Avenue and students at the middle school during dismissal time. Respondents felt that there should be some means for merchants to talk to administrators about the problem and offer input on policies that might improve the situation.

When asked about the strengths Mount Vernon possessed that could be used as resources to build their ideal school, 27 percent of respondents cited the diversity of its people. The Mount Vernon community was described as a microcosm of the global economy. Respondents felt that this strength offers the opportunity for diversity of thought on how to best prepare young children for the challenges of the twenty-first century. The city's small-town nature was cited as an asset by 22 percent of respondents. Although it is urban, respondents describe it as having a small and intimate setting with its small political and physical infrastructure making it easy for things to get done. For example, the mayor and the city council operate very closely to the people they serve, and residents enjoy the local government's open-door policy. As a result, many long-term relationships have been established over the years, as was reflected in the 17 percent of people who also said that people caring about one another was an asset. Many thought this closeness would bode well for solving complex and sensitive future problems.

Some 17 percent of respondents mentioned Mount Vernon's access to valuable human capital as an asset. The city is unique in that there are many successful people who live in Mount Vernon, having made a conscious decision to remain there in spite the problems the city faces. In addition, there are many people who have moved away, and have gone on to achieve national and international fame. However, many continue to return to the city because they recognize it as their home. Respondents believed that this resource could be used to help Mount Vernon rebuild its schools.

Chapter 8

Public Dissatisfaction with the District's Performance on Student Achievement

Most of the people interviewed were quick to talk about the many good things taking place within the school district that go unrecognized. They spoke about the district's number of dedicated administrators and teachers who possess years of experience in public education. At the elementary school level, the district earned a great many accolades. Several respondents went as far as singling out Traphagan and Lincoln Elementary Schools as schools of excellence that fit criteria for their ideal school. Respondents also spoke well of the many students at the high school who did well and went on to Ivy League colleges. Many respondents, including youth who were interviewed, agreed that quality education is available for students who are eager and interested in learning. Although most respondents admitted that learning is taking place within the Mount Vernon School District, 75 percent of those who answered the question described the district as having either a poor or mixed performance (see Table 8.1).

Of the respondents, 28 percent expressed mixed reviews on the district's performance. They gave high scores to advances made at the elementary-school level. Their dissatisfaction was primarily with Mount Vernon's middle and high schools. In addition to pointing to dismal performances on standardized test scores and low graduation rates, respondents expressed particular concern about the overall sense of an unsafe and disorderly learning environment. Respondents pointed to a prepon-

Table 8.1

Responses to the Question: "Does the Mount Vernon School District Prepare Students for the Future?"

	Stakeholder Group				
Prepares for Future	**Specialist**	**CBO**	**CAL**	**Influentials**	**Total**
Yes	6 %	3 %	6 %	3 %	18 %
No	10 %	19 %	8 %	8 %	45 %
Mixed: Elementary, Yes	10 %	6 %	7 %	6 %	29 %
Mixed: Other	3 %	0 %	4 %	1 %	8 %
Total	29 %	28 %	25 %	18 %	100 %

derance of evidence demonstrating the district's mixed performance. First, they mentioned the many parents who elect not to send their children to the district's schools after the sixth grade. Fear of violence at the secondary school level has convinced those parents, who could afford the choice, to select alternative schools for their children. Students who leave the district after elementary school are often the district's higher-performing learners. This phenomenon, which respondents describe as *bright flight*, drains the system of its stronger students, leaving the district with the lowest performing students with the greatest needs. One district administrator estimated the loss of as many as 25 to 30 percent of students who do not show up for enrollment in the district's middle schools after having completed the elementary grades. Educators are faced with the formidable task of teaching the children who remain, many of whom have a multitude of educational challenges.

Second, respondents pointed to the influx of non-residents who enter the district. In search of better schools, parents from the Bronx cross Mount Vernon borders to be able to use a Mount Vernon address in order to enroll their children in Mount Vernon schools. These students have often not had the strong elementary training from which local students have benefited. These students enter the district, often unprepared for the rigor of a higher-performing district. Third, the district has a large and growing student population of English Language Learners. With the influx of a growing immigrant population, educators are forced to allocate a tremendous amount of resources to support these students. In addition, the district has an estimated 15 to 18 percent of students who are classified as "children with special needs," who also require significant amounts of special help to succeed. Finally, respondents expressed concern about the many parents who discontinue their involvement in school activities after their children complete elementary school. That is a time when peer pressure and the rapid maturation of students would require parents to be deeply involved in their children's lives. Instead, their support diminishes, leaving educators, administrators, and students to deal with a multitude of problems on their own.

Respondents who felt that the district, on the whole, was not preparing Mount Vernon's youth for their future, raised concerns not only about problems at the secondary levels, but also about children's not being prepared at the elementary grade levels as well. This group represented 47 percent of all respondents who answered the question (see Table 9). Interestingly, respondents were very critical of policies set by the federal government's *2001 No Child Left Behind* (NCLB) law, and the way it has changed elementary school curriculum. They spoke about children, even at high performing elementary schools, who are no longer learning the basic skills needed for critical thinking. Instead, respondents asserted, Mount Vernon's children were becoming experts in taking tests. The parent of a first grader in an elementary school on the north side captured the sentiments of many respondents who expressed dissatisfaction with the district's performance:

> I think teaching is definitely different than where we were in our day. Even the wording is different. The expectations are different. I think they're expecting more from our children and putting much stress on our children. I think it's breaking self-esteem. I think we've created a No Child Left Behind of tracking; and I think that the tracking is to our demise. I really believe that my daughter is going into second—she just completed the first grade. No, she's not taking the test but they are preparing them. They are preparing them and they're using terms which I think are not appropriate at the kindergarten/first level. They're using the terms "midterm." They're doing finals! That's what they are giving these kids at the first-grade level. Don't call it midterm! You know, we get into that at high school and college. Don't call it a final, and I as a parent have to watch my stress level and her stress level because we can't put that on our children at such a young age . . . I always—we look at the short-term and it's great—we can say at the elementary school level, our children are achieving and Mount Vernon is competing. I want that kind of school system for my child. But, at

> the same time, what happens when she leaves that school and you're basing everything on these tests? Have we really done the work that they were supposed to do?

This sentiment was also expressed by education specialists at the middle-school level. They were candid with their thoughts on the extent to which children coming from the elementary schools lacked the comprehension skills needed for critical thinking.

Many respondents suggested that the pressures posed by the demand to pass standardized tests, coupled with the lack of resources for early intervention for children who struggle with their basic skills, make it virtually impossible for most students to have an overall successful educational experience. Respondents believed that students do well at the elementary school level, but the vast majority of those who remain within the district beyond the sixth grade lack the critical skills to do well at the secondary school level. These perceptions were echoed by respondents from the business community. They describe high school students as unprepared for the workforce, lacking the ability to fill out simple application forms. Writing samples suggest many students lack even basic English language skills. These factors suggest that much needs to be done to create a learning environment that will meet the public's expectations for higher performing schools.

Chapter 9

Major Problems Facing the District

The Absence of a Safe Place for Students to Learn

The perception of unsafe schools and the absence of social order were characterized most often as a major problem threatening the district; they were cited by 42 percent of respondents who answered the question (see Table 9.1). The district's history of violence continues to shape people's negative perceptions, especially of the high school. Some respondents recalled stories about sexual assaults that took place in the 1980s.

Several respondents argued that the problem was not as severe as others believed, but that the district was a victim of biased press coverage. Although most respondents agreed that violence at the high school is exaggerated by the media, the absence of safety and social order is perceived as a real issue within the district. Several respondents suggested that administrators are in denial about the extent to which safety is a problem. Because of this, they often minimize the crisis. An elected government official describes how administrators fail to do all they can to create a safe environment within the district:

> I'm aware that one of the complaints that the police department has is that the school district does not communicate, even when there's an immediate issue requiring police presence. They don't call the police or they like to portray it as having happened in the park, not in the school, certainly, although it's between the two kids who are from the same school and it probably started in the school and culminated after

school outside. They take no responsibility. And they almost hinder the investigation.

Table 9.1

Responses to the Question: "What is the Most Important Problem Facing Mount Vernon Public Schools?"

Most Important Problem	Stakeholder Group				
	Specialist	CBO	CAL	Influentials	Total
Lack of Safety/ Social Order	8 %	12 %	15 %	7 %	42 %
Lack of Parent Participation	3 %	1 %	1 %	1 %	6 %
Lack of Adequate Learning Environment	3 %	7 %	1 %	4 %	15 %
Low Teacher Quality	4 %	0 %	0 %	1 %	5 %
Lack of Leadership	7 %	5 %	4 %	1 %	17 %
Lack of Funding/ Inequitable Funding	6 %	3 %	1 %	1 %	11 %
Apathy	0 %	0 %	1 %	0 %	1 %
Other	0 %	3 %	0 %	0 %	3 %
Total	31 %	31 %	23 %	15 %	100 %

Several administrators, teachers, and students interviewed concurred that crime on school property has been blown out of proportion and that most of the crime that does take place starts in the community.

Regardless of where the problem begins, respondents believed that schools are unsafe, and that administrators should be more aggressive in enforcing a no-tolerance policy. Several respondents suggested that the absence of safety and order continues to exist due to the unwillingness on the part of administrators to approach the crisis as a systemic problem. Instead, the approaches administrators take are often short-term solutions. For example, some respondents complained about the district's failure to enforce policies that are already in place to handle issues of violence and disorder. They described instances where students had been removed from the class by the teacher and/or suspended by the principal for inappropriate behavior. As opposed to administrators reinforcing decisions made at the building level, they have been known to reverse decisions and instruct building leaders to readmit the students. Efforts to appease a disgruntled parent—or someone with political connections—leave educators and building leaders in a quandary when administrators at the central office yield to political pressure by rescinding a decision. This has resulted in allowing students with multiple infractions to remain in the classroom, and to cause further disruptions. Although yielding to political pressure may offer short-term solutions to complex problems, some respondents suggest that it is short-sighted in that it often creates a culture of perceived tolerance.

There is also an unsettled philosophical difference on how to handle students who misbehave. Some suggest that children often act out as a way to seek help. They have multiple problems and often no family support at home. Since schools are the only safe haven for these youngsters, some believe that suspension is not the answer. To eject these vulnerable youngsters from school for misbehavior could sometimes be the impetus for a life critically deferred. Others concurred, but still believed that allowing a few disruptive students to remain in the classroom puts the majority of students at risk. Many respondents pointed out the lack of meaningful alternative settings for these young students. Although emotions ran high on these two perspectives, most people agreed that there were no easy answers to this complex problem. However, many noted that the absence of a resolution to this problem creates an environment for unsafe and disorderly buildings. In addition, it fosters the perception that there is a high tolerance for disorder.

There were those respondents who believed that the absence of safety was indeed a community problem and that it was unfair to hold the district accountable. Many describe, for example, the state of denial among parents who are unwilling to admit the extent to which their children are involved in gang-related activities. Respondents discussed their concerns about adults who themselves participate in gang activities, presenting negative role models to young children. They describe the absence of positive role models with high ethical standards who had been so important in past generations.

There were ministers who suggested that, more often than not, youngsters who are involved in these behaviors are not part of their church congregation. Many of their parishioners either live outside of the district, or send their children to private schools. Although several churches were working to combat violence among youth, some of these ministers gave the sense that there was a clear distinction between their congregation and "those other kids" involved in violence and crime. However, there were a few who acknowledged that crime was a community-wide problem. One minister shared what he had recently said to his congregation about crime being a community problem:

> I stood up in the congregation a few months ago, and declared that the problem in our city has nothing to do with the mayor and has nothing to do with the superintendent of schools. You know, shooting and the violence and that nonsense. I spoke to every parent in the community. I said, "This is our problem." I said, "We have created this monster." Parents. And that's the clergymen's responsibility. It's not their responsibility to raise our children and teach them that it's wrong to shoot a gun. "That's not mine," I says, "it's a parental responsibility. We stand up and we blame everyone else," I says. So this lawlessness and recklessness is really coming to roost. [A] generation of babies raising babies, the issue of marriage, this, that, and the other. Family, how to raise it—I've got parenting classes here. How to raise a child.

Respondents spoke emotionally about the absence of safety and social order within the schools. Although many suggested the district needed to adopt a no-tolerance policy, most seemed to feel that it was a complex problem and that the at-large community needed to play a greater role in finding a solution.

The Absence of Leadership Within the District and Beyond

The second most important problem facing the district, as identified by 24 percent of respondents, was the absence of leadership. (See Table 9.2)

Several respondents spoke of the great victory won when the Black community seized political control of the school system. The 1980s posed a real opportunity for the community to use its political capital to build a national model for urban education. Instead, respondents described how elected leaders became entwined in petty politics and ended up being no different then the regime they had overthrown. A prominent leader in the community discusses the missed opportunity for building a world-class education system. Instead, he claimed, leaders created a vision for mediocrity and maintaining the status-quo:

> No, we can't blame anybody for this mess. We've created this mess. This is not [Name's] fault. Schools were better [then]. And that's the truth. We won't say that. We'll jump up and down, throw statistics around—but we missed the moment. And I think the moment was that we had an opportunity to shift the paradigm, and the money took us. I says, "What are you guys doing?" I says, "You're gonna get a chance to make history, and the first thing you wanna do is what we always do, slavery's done a job on us." It's done a job on us. And I said, "Wow. This is all we know how to do."

Table 9.2

Responses to the Question: "What is the Second Most Important Problem Facing Mount Vernon Public Schools?"

	Stakeholder Group				
Second Most Important Problem	**Specialist**	**CBO**	**CAL**	**Influentials**	**Total**
Lack of Safety/ Social Order	12 %	5 %	5 %	2 %	24 %
Lack of Parent Participation	0 %	3 %	3 %	4 %	10 %
Lack of Adequate Learning Environment	0 %	5 %	3 %	5 %	13 %
Low Teacher Quality	2 %	2 %	5 %	5 %	14 %
Lack of Leadership	14 %	7 %	3 %	0 %	24 %
Lack of Funding/ Inequitable Funding	2 %	4 %	2 %	0 %	8 %
Apathy	0 %	2 %	2 %	3 %	7 %
Other	0 %	0 %	0 %	0 %	0 %
Total	30 %	28 %	23 %	19 %	100 %

The respondent goes on to discuss the community's rejection of the best and brightest candidates for leadership, and that politics has allowed the community to accept so little for their young people.

Some respondents pointed out that although the composition of the board is gradually changing, people who were elected because of their roles as advocates still largely comprise its membership. They were chosen in a time when the community mobilized around the issue of greater representation and people were elected based on their ability to advocate for that cause. They were not elected for their expertise in education or for running a multimillion-dollar agency. An elected official went on to question whether the board possesses the skill set needed to lead the district in the twenty-first century:

> I think that for the district to be successful, people have to feel that the people on the board are either educators or are in [possession] of a set of managerial and professional skills that can move the district forward. And I think to the extent that people associate the [current] board members with community activism, and I guess I'm distinguishing that from civic involvement—but in terms of righting a social wrong, as opposed to civic involvement, which is imparting civic concern to the institution—the board is kind of seen as an instrument, an agent of change, and not as a managerial board. I think that it's gonna be difficult to bring citywide buy-in to the district.

Although well-intentioned, hardworking people have volunteered a great deal of time as trustees, they are perceived by many respondents as lacking the vision and skills needed to lead the district. Effective twenty-first century leadership will require higher levels of competence.

Instead of serving as a visionary body, respondents suggest that the present board micromanages, while demonstrating little or no educational expertise. As a result, superintendents have been marginalized by a board that fails to understand that its role is to set policy and allow the professionals to run day-to-day operations. An education specialist and longtime resident described the effects of this lack of leadership:

> I went for, let's put [it], qualified, competent people, and they still don't understand the role of the board. The superintendent is the board's CEO, who's supposed to be running the schools. They get involved in minor things that have nothing to do with them. They picked the superintendent to run the schools, and they actually are running the school and the superintendent sometimes is running into a stone wall. The superintendent has expertise in education and everything else, and he's trying to placate everybody on this board to get something through, which is totally ridiculous, and I think that that's the main problem.

Respondents describe one trickle-down effect this micromanagement has had on the district: high turnover rates at the building level, especially at the high school. Respondents said that an environment where administrators at the district's highest levels are forced to placate the board in order to get things done has a *domino effect* upon all levels of management and of the teaching staff. The superintendent placates the board, principals placate the superintendent, and teachers placate the principals. Decisions are often based on political expedience, rather than on the best interests of the children.

Several respondents spoke of the highly-charged political environment in which education professionals are forced to work. This, coupled with the constant influx of new building leaders with varying leadership styles, has resulted in the premature retirement of dedicated and experienced professionals, which drains the system of valuable expertise. Several education professionals describe their painful decision to leave prematurely, in spite of their love for their students. One teacher who recently retired from the district described how a change in leadership made her decide to leave:

> I loved Mount Vernon; I loved the kids in Mount Vernon. My children said, "Mom, can't you get a job?" I could, but I don't want to, because my heart is in Mount Vernon, it's where my children were born; it's where they started out. The only teaching job I ever had, and I love those kids, I love them because they have such soul, and they're so vibrant, but the kids in Mount Vernon, they're so real. And I love them, and I miss them. Right until we got a new principal and things started to change. Her values and mine were not the same, and I did not feel supported by her, and I'm a very strong teacher and I felt there was animosity there. And I just didn't feel supported. I felt like anything I tried to do that required disciplining the children, she balked, and I think there was a bit of a race issue there, I would say, the first time I've ever confronted that anywhere, and it was bothersome to me.

Several respondents suggested that the turnover in staff reflects the board's weak leadership, as well as its inability to create an inspiring work environment. Some suggest that board actions perpetuate an environment of retribution. As a result, people who work in the district are distracted from what should be their main concern—teaching children. Instead, they devote their attention to searching for political cover, placating superiors, and—more and more—making decisions and judgments that are politically expedient. Instead of getting bogged down in such a political quagmire, some professionals simply decide to leave.

There was the sense that the public does not recognize that the public schools are the responsibility of the entire community. Respondents suggested that residents view public schools, and all their problems, as the responsibility of the Black community. Some suggested it was a result of a lack of leadership at the board level. They described behaviors of some board members that contribute to this public perception. Their actions suggest that they are at the helm of an institution that belongs to the Black community and not the community-at-large. For example, respondents described how members of the board have openly displayed racial bias in their search for candidates to fill positions in the district. A White resident described what many other respondents expressed:

> And then the other issue is, you can't, and I hope I'm gonna say this right, you can't go into the newspaper and say, "I wanna Black person for this position." You gotta go into the newspaper and say, "I want the most qualified person for this position." They've done it, they're on record as doing that, you know, and it's wrong. They used to say the same thing about the ICA.

Respondents, Black and White, across all stakeholder groups, described a history of overt intolerance to White people who lived in the community or worked within the district. They described a history of disregarding the opinions put forth by people who happened to be White. There were references made about a proposal for a charter school, which had been turned down, largely because it was introduced by members of the White community. Another reference also was made about a proposal to expand the Pennington School to K-8. Some suggested that race played a factor in turning down this proposal. Another pattern that respondents claimed is tolerated is a frequent suggestion that problems with the teaching staff are caused only by White educators. The following statement from a Black educator offers an opinion on this matter:

> From the standpoint of educating the students, the teachers at [Mount Vernon High School] are some of the most professional, and this is—I'll have to say this with regards to caring about other school districts because I have not been in a different school district—teachers at other school districts, who have talked with or met with [Mount Vernon High School teachers], [have] told me that [Mount Vernon High School

> teachers] are some of the best in Westchester County. Now, I wasn't asking them if this was the case. Unsolicited, they just told me that was the case. I kind of have a feel for who's not doing the job and who's lax, and who doesn't really want to be there, and as I began looking closer at the teachers, again, especially in the [name] department, I'm saying, "Wow, these teachers are giving all that they know how to these students." There've been charges that, because some of the teachers are White, they're not doing all that they could and should do. I have not found that to be the case, I have not.

> I've heard this many times over the last three years, in particular, that the [Mount Vernon High School] teachers are maligned because of whatever, and I'm saying, "Well, is that in fact the case?" I have not found that to be the case. And I would not, I would not be providing this kind of opinion if I thought it was. If I thought it was the case, then I would definitely, definitely say it is, but it just gets—especially when it comes to the divide between the Black teachers and the White teachers, in terms of what one brings versus the other. Unfortunately, I've found there are more Black teachers who have a more casual attitude than a lot of, a lot of the White teachers.

According to school administrators, as of January 2008, the total number of employees was 1,961. Blacks represent 60.27 percent of the administration and 33 percent of the teaching staff. Although great improvement has been made integrating the administrative level, integration at the teaching level continues to lag, with more minorities filling positions at the assistant teacher level. For example, while Blacks represent 33% of the teaching staff, they represent almost 70% of the assistant teaching positions—the lowest faculty level in the district.[1]

There was no respondent, Black or White, who was not supportive of the need to aggressively recruit people of color to fill important positions within the district. Several respondents even questioned why the teaching staff continued to be racially imbalanced, given the number of students of color enrolled in the district. There were also no respondents who denied the need to weed out many educators who are either *burned out* or who lack the sensitivity or interest to teach children. The concern expressed by many who responded was that staff members were not always being judged by their performance, but by whom they knew. For example, some respondents suggested that there were occasions where incompetence was overlooked or favoritism shown for staff persons who had the right connections, knew the right people, or had been in the right sorority or fraternity. Respondents expressed a desire to move away from this pattern and begin to hold everyone in the district accountable to higher standards and levels of excellence. They desired accountability based on helping students achieve their highest potential, rather than on whom someone knows or the color of one's skin.

There were those who spoke about how this environment was a result of the political backlash that resonated from the years of inequity imposed on the Black community by the actions of the Italian Civic Association (ICA). Some respondents described the board's lack of leadership—its inability to move the district to a higher level of excellence. They felt the board should govern in the best interest of all citizens, and not just for those citizens who have been previously disenfranchised. Failing to do so has helped create the perception that public schools and all their problems belong to the Black community. Almost all of the people interviewed who spoke about this topic felt that this political backlash has gone on too long. Rather than inspiring unified public support for the district, the board continues to operate as if it represents one constituency group. This, many suggested, continues the polarization that has existed over the years. This kind of leadership at the board level has created a crisis in the district.

Finally, respondents spoke of a lack of leadership in the community at large. They spoke of the time when the community arose in support of public schools. People from all segments of the community stood up against an inequitable system and demanded quality education for all children. This level of leadership has been displayed throughout the history of Mount Vernon, but especially in the 1960s, during the Civil Rights Movement, and in the 1980s, during the battle with the ICA for broader representation of Blacks in policy-making decisions. Many described the absence of a strong middle-class who would demand excellence in education. One respondent used the City of New Rochelle to illustrate the value of leadership within the at-large community and what it could do for a city like Mount Vernon:

> I try hard not to always use this as a reference point, but I grew up in New Rochelle. It was economically, ethnically, the whole thing was quite different over there. You know, about 30 percent of the people in New Rochelle are African American and there is a large Italian community, a large Jewish community, and certainly nothing's perfect, even in New Rochelle. But the power base of the schools in New

> Rochelle was the PTA. PTA was like a little mob. It was cliquish, hard to get in, probably hard to stay in, I suspect, but they consistently drove excellence into those schools. And they were a farm team for the school board. They knew how to organize, how to run campaigns, they knew how to raise money. Heaven forbid you didn't like something they were doing, you had a real problem on your hands, and I'm not necessarily saying that we need to create a kabala in Mount Vernon to match the PTA in New Rochelle, but you need something like that.

Respondents felt that leadership is lacking at all levels, including the community at large. It would be in everyone's best interest to find ways to develop a school system that would attract and maintain a strong middle-class population. There was much discussion about the overall absence of popular participation in matters of public education. The middle-class population in Mount Vernon has distanced itself from the education debate and, as a result, the entire community has suffered. There was also discussion of the many other legitimate priorities people have and how difficult it is for poor people to get involved. Given the high correlation between strong public school systems and high property values, the lack of interest from the middle-class community—particularly the Black middle class—was extremely puzzling. Mount Vernon has the largest percentage of middle-class Blacks in the entire region. They do not suffer the economic oppression that is a reality for many families in the city. Respondents suggested that the absence of leadership voices from the middle class, both Black and White, is deafening. It is time for true educational leadership to emerge.

Chapter 10

No Trust in the Process for Decision Making

Respondents were asked to select which statement most closely reflected their opinion: (a) through a formal process like the office of the superintendent and the school board, (b) behind closed doors, (c) by a combination of the two, or (d) things don't get done. Most respondents, 49 percent of those who answered the question, believed things get done behind closed doors, and 30 percent of respondents believed things get done through a combination of a formal process and behind closed doors. Only 9 percent believed that things do not get done at all. The majority of respondents, 59.6 percent, believed that the process of decision-making fails to evoke a high level of public trust, and it does not stand the test for good fiduciary oversight. See Tables 10.1 and 10.2.

There were those respondents who believed that the office of the superintendent and the school board are the appropriate channels for conducting business. They recognized that the board has a responsibility to understand how and what business is being conducted, and that abiding by a formal process is good business practice. These respondents also believed that making decisions behind closed doors is an appropriate and necessary way of doing business. A building leader described the value of such a dual process:

> Well, let me put it this way; there are some things that need to be done through the board. There are some things that need to be done through the superintendent, and there are some things that need to be done through a combination, and there's certainly some things that need to

be done behind closed doors. It is not always necessary or it is not always in the best interest to have everything out there that's gonna happen. Simple reason is you have five different factors and if everybody starts jumping in, nothing gets done. Sometimes, the leadership has to take the bull by the horn and say this is how we gonna do it. I firmly believe in leadership being active and not autocratic, but certainly knows who is, where the buck stops.

Table 10.1
Responses to the Question: "How Do Things Get Done for Public Education in Mount Vernon?"

	Stakeholder Group				
Key Elements	**Specialist**	**CBO**	**CAL**	**Influentials**	**Total**
Formal Process	8 %	3 %	0 %	0 %	11 %
Behind Closed Doors	7 %	7 %	11 %	5 %	30 %
Combination	8 %	20 %	8 %	13 %	49 %
Things Don't Get Done	3 %	2 %	5 %	0 %	10 %
Total	26 %	32 %	24 %	18 %	100 %

Table 10.2
Responses to the Question: "Is that a good thing?" (A Follow-Up Question to, "How Do Things Get Done for Public Education in Mount Vernon?")

	Stakeholder Group				
Key Elements	**Specialist**	**CBO**	**CAL**	**Influentials**	**Total**
No	13 %	19 %	23 %	4 %	59 %
Yes	11 %	9 %	3 %	4 %	27 %
Sometimes	4 %	6 %	0 %	4 %	14 %
Neutral	0 %	0 %	0 %	0 %	0 %
Total	28 %	34 %	26 %	12 %	100 %

Even though there were those respondents who described a dual process that works, most described a decision-making process that undermines the confidence of the public. Things that do get done through the formal process are described by some respondents as cumbersome and too difficult to involve the public. Although the respondents felt the board meetings had gotten better over the past two years, they continue to take an inordinate amount of time to conduct business. Respondents described board meetings that go on until twelve o'clock at night before agenda items that parents are passionate about are addressed. Parents become wary and find it difficult to participate while at the same time having to worry about getting home to their children.

There were those who felt the formal process made it difficult to conduct business. For example, there were some administrators who discussed their frustration with having to bring everything before the board. Although they acknowledged the need for a formal process, they questioned the extent to which the board has to get involved in every minute detail on all decision-making. It slows the process to a degree that affects conditions at the school-building level.

The vast majority of respondents described a formal process as little more than a façade, since by the time most issues get to the board and to the public, decisions have already been made. They provided specific examples of how some decisions appear to be based on cronyism, favoritism, or influences from the outside—such decisions are vetted and decided long before they come to a public meeting. For members of the public who have access to decision making, like the PTA members, respondents felt there was a better understanding of what goes into decision making and, as a result, had somewhat more confidence in the process. But, in general, respondents had their reservations about a process that takes place primarily behind closed doors. One public administrator summed up the sentiments of many respondents:

> I think it all happens behind closed doors. I think that the public face of the school board endorses what has already been pre-determined beforehand. And I think if you did a poll in this city, you'd find that there's an overwhelming sentiment, and maybe other places as well too, I think there is a sense that in many school districts, especially you go to the school board meetings kind of pro forma, there's very little dissension because a lot of dissension takes place at the work sessions, and that may be the case, but I think here, I think there's a handful of people who really kind of orchestrate the direction the district goes in. And I don't think it's educators.

One of the disadvantages expressed by this respondent was the lost opportunity on the part of the board to draw upon experts who could prove valuable to good decision-making. The board would be more effective if it surrounded itself with experts to help guide good decision-making. A discussion with a high-ranking public official described the opportunity cost for conducting business behind closed doors:

> When things get done behind closed doors, I think you short-cut the process, the vetting process. . . . Sometimes we make decisions and on paper or in a vacuum, it sounds fabulous. You know, we're going to put a curfew on, I don't know, on children age 12 and age 16 and under or whatever. But what happens is the way our society works is, there's always a way around it. And what you do here bulges out into something else totally unexpected. And I think when you do things behind closed doors and you don't have vetting process hearings, experts coming in to explain what are the consequences of these things, I think you're bound to fail. One example I can think of is years ago, there was a push to take, to make the elementary schools go up to grade eight. And that was really coming from the Pennington School District, because those parents wanted to keep their kids together as long as possible and put off the inevitability of private school. Well, at the time, this school district and the majority of the people of the city were opposed to that, because they felt that it was just a ploy on their part to create this private little environment. And now that's what we're doing. And so I think you need to have—I'm a believer in getting expert opinions, getting consultants to come in who have studied things and who have a full understanding of what the . . . how is this gonna affect what you do? And what potential do you see here? You gotta put—you have to put that all together in an open environment.

Overwhelmingly, respondents described the practice of operating behind closed doors as a broken process for decision-making that does not bode well for public confidence. The formal processes in place were perceived as either cumbersome or *window dressing* for decisions that are made behind closed doors and influenced by political factors.

Chapter 11

A Public Disconnected and Disenfranchised

Representatives from business and civic organizations spoke about the many volunteer groups who mentor and raise monies for scholarships for outstanding students going on to colleges and universities. Among the respondents, 64 percent believed their personal relationship with the district or their organization's relationship with the district is either *very good* or *improved* in recent years. They described great strides made in how administrators work with the public. This newfound regard for the public was described by some as a welcome sign.

However, when asked how they perceived the general public and its relationship with the district, respondents described a relationship reminiscent of the one the public had with the board when it was controlled by the Italian Civic Association (ICA). There is an underlying assumption on the part of the public that the board is controlled by outside influences and that decisions are made based on politics, not on what is in the best interest of the children. Some described a closed environment within which school politics are played out perpetuating an aura of suspicion. Whether these perceptions are real or imagined, a closed-door policy has resulted in a public that is disillusioned with its leaders. It fosters the notion that access is only available to those who know the right people. A sense of betrayal pervades the entire atmosphere. Consequently, there is very little meaningful dialogue between the general public and the school district. A leader of a community-based organization described his disappointment with the board of trustees in the following way:

> . . . And we put these people in with the intention that, when they get there, to help it grow. But once a person is there, they change. They say you got me here, but they don't even know who you are. You can't even get in to see these people.

Some suggest that, as a result of this closed political environment, there is a disgruntled public. This sentiment was shared across all socioeconomic lines. People have been turned off to school politics. They have become disengaged and have redirected their energies into what is most familiar—their own struggle for survival. Although this concern was raised by many groups, the Black community was particularly critical. A parent who was involved with CEPAA described her sense of betrayal by people she elected to represent her:

> I used to go make phone calls and everything. But the thing about it is a lot of people that got elected let us down. And when that happens, when the people let you down—the people that you fight to get in office let you down—then it's a big problem. Like, nobody wants to leave work after working 8 to 10 hours a day, or in my case sometimes I work from 9 to 2 in the morning. Nine [in the morning] to 2 in the morning. And I'm gonna leave work and go sit in CEPAA and pack envelopes and stuff like that. And you're promising me this. So now I feel like, well, what the hell am I voting for [name] for [what]? Or this one promised to fix the schools, but when they got in there—and let's say they promised to get every kid English books. Well, when you got in there, English books was the furthest thing from a thought that you could have because you've got windows and this, but before you come back to the community that elected you and explain that, "Look, before I can get your school English books, I've got to get a roof put on the building" or "I've got to do X, Y, Z" or "I've got to make a classroom for your child to sit in with their English book." And these things never came back and being explained to people; so people feel jilted. That's how I feel about it.

Although many respondents describe the important and effective role United Black Clergy (UBC) has played in reshaping the education landscape in Mount Vernon, most suggest that in recent years, the churches' actions have been self-serving. Some suggested the churches' ability to mobilize their congregations has led to people being voted into office who are not the best leaders for the community. Churches were also criticized for not looking beyond their own congregations for talented people to fill important positions in the district.

In essence, the UBC is perceived by some segments in the community as the new Black Italian Civic Association (ICA)—a well-oiled political machine that uses the district as its political pawn. One leader in the community summed it up this way: "We bought into the ICA's system. We just changed faces. We're doing the same thing, just changing faces. You know, giving out jobs, setting up families for the rest of their life, dot dot dot." Some respondents suggested that this political environment has strained the relationship between the public and its school district, which is reflected in a public that is reluctant to get more involved. Some spoke about the difficulty for the Black community to be critical of its Black leaders, publicly or privately. Some are especially hesitant to speak out against their religious leaders. In some circles, speaking out against the Black clergy, in particular, is viewed as sacrilegious. A religious leader spoke about this dilemma:

> Yeah, we're silent. Because they're people that are placed there by our religious institutions, by our religious leaders, by people that we revere. And the injustices, unfairness of the—it just kind of goes undealt with. "Oh, it's just politics." We kind of deal with it like that. But we have been silent. And we haven't put enough pressure on them to perform. And what is happened, is the office of the superintendent has become a scapegoat for their responsibility. We elected you to make sure that we have great schools, and you keep blaming superintendent and replacing one as the answer. No, we need to replace you. Small-town syndrome: We like people no matter how good or bad they perform. And we're Black. We're Black. That's who we are. But that's a major piece, and that doesn't help the process any.

Instead of speaking out, people simply choose to stay away. Those who elect to be involved do so with an aura of suspicion. They question the motives of well-intentioned people and operate in cliques to such an extent that it makes true partnering impossible.

One respondent suggested that the attitude on the part of the board and some administrators contributes to the poor relationship between the public and the district. They do not go far enough to encourage true public engagement. For example, although the relationship between the public and the public school district is weak, some respondents suggested that there are people who are interested in becoming involved.

However, they stop short of taking an active role. Unaware of how to become meaningfully involved, the public has become frustrated with the process. An educator described a public in search of a place on the political landscape:

> I think that whereas there are some who at least would like to make it a stronger one, probably don't know how to do that or have been frustrated in their attempts to make stronger ties with the school district. And so the overall effect, in my view, is that, you know, the public is kind of sitting out there, the school district is kind of doing their thing and saying, "We really don't care what you think. We are the educators, we know what's best. So we're gonna do our thing." And again, I get back to, not only in terms of businesses having an input in terms of policy, the public has, I think, a legitimate voice in terms of policy, in terms of schools and what they do. But it's not there.

One of the respondents, a pastor of a local church congregation, described how he had hoped to work with the district. He withdrew his support when it became clear to him that what he had envisioned was not what was envisioned by school administrators. This sentiment was expressed by several respondents—they felt pigeonholed into meaningless roles administrators wanted them to play in the district versus roles that evolve from a collaborative model.

Interviews with administrators at the central office revealed that few resources are applied to promoting parent and community involvement. For example, there is no full-time person at the cabinet level who is devoted to building community relations and building support for parent involvement. There was a person responsible for Title I programs, which include community and parent involvement. However, that person was also responsible for grants administration and administering the lottery process for the entire district. There is an administrator responsible for outreach under a federally funded program entitled *Safe Schools for Health Children Project*. In addition to staff support, there is a board member who was assigned to chair the Parent Outreach Committee in her capacity as a non-paid volunteer.

There was no evidence of paid parent advocates at the school-building level to support the outreach efforts of the principal, other than PTA parent volunteers. Itemized budgets on Title I expenditures support this observation. They show dollars that had been slated for parent involvement initiatives having gone unused and rolled over for multiple years. There also was no evidence of the capacity for outreach to non-English-speaking families. For example, in spite of the growing number of non-English-speaking families, there is no institutionalized process for translating and disseminating written materials. Administrators admit to a lack of investment in resources for community engagement. They described the difficult task of juggling multiple priorities. Administrators highlight Parent Involvement Day as one of the programs the district sponsors to encourage broader public participation. Although respondents recognized that administrators have to make difficult decisions about priorities, they wanted more resources to be invested in improving the relationship between the district and the public.

There are those respondents who describe a disenfranchised population who are simply struggling on a day-to-day basis and have little time to show their support for public education. They work multiple jobs and do not see traditional involvement as relevant to the many other legitimate priorities they have. A leader of a local community-based organization described the difficulty of becoming involved:

> So you've got people now paying exorbitant amounts to keep a roof over their head, but they don't have access to living-wage jobs. Then tie in to that, you're right, I believe that education is a proper way out and people should be organizing around educational issues, but people were so burdened by cost of living, just making ends meet, putting food on the table, paying the rent. A lot of people's civic capacity is somewhat limited. I always—I like to say housing and security underlie all other economic and security issues. When people are desperate, working two to three jobs, it affects their ability in their jobs, just to pay the rent. We have to work 60–70 hours to pay rent that affects their ability to perform in their jobs, if they're going to school in addition to that. But, more importantly, to participate in community activities, to do community improvement, to organize, to create better services, create a greater democracy. They're very limited to do that. When you're working two to three jobs, how are you going to be able to participate in extra-curricular activities, like organizing for better school services, for better education?

At best, community members are described as *reactive*, willing to mobilize when something goes very wrong or if it relates to a problem with their own child. Public perception of this group and their relation with the district is one of complete disconnect.

Respondents describe another disenfranchised population consisting of members of the bedroom community who have absolutely no use for, or interest in, the public schools within the district. They have no intention of using the public schools for their children, or they are older adults who have already gone through the system and have adult children who live outside the district. They make no correlation between paying taxes and the sense of duty that comes with ownership of local public institutions. Some are described by respondents as even being embarrassed by living in a community with a school system that offers so little return for their investment. Others are described as formerly active citizens who have been beaten by the Black political power base. They care about local public schools, but have grown wary of being exposed to the political backlash to which they were subjected for so many years.

Respondents were sensitive to the board's tremendous task of rebuilding an institution that is bankrupt because of years of neglect. One respondent pointed out that the public has failed to recognize this difficulty. Another respondent thought it was unfortunate that blaming board trustees has become such a favorite sport for many citizens. The level of hostility and disenfranchisement has become so pronounced that the public is often oblivious to the many successes that have achieved over the years. The completion of major capital improvement projects, the institution of a district-wide curriculum, significant improvements in student performance on state-standardized test scores are among the many achievements within the district under the guidance of the board of trustees. However, it has not been enough to rebuild public confidence. To the extent that the chasm widens between the public and the school district, it will continue to be to the detriment of its children.

Chapter 12

Who Owns Public Schools?

This study was based on the assumption that all public institutions belong to the public and were established by the public to achieve desirable public outcomes. In other words, every person is a legitimate owner of all public institutions, including public schools. This is not to suggest that all individuals want to—or should—be involved in their day-to-day operations. Rather, citizens should be at the forefront of shaping a vision for public schools—one that represents the community's shared beliefs on how to prepare children to become productive members of society and future guardians of our democratic institutions. It also is based on the assumption that ownership of public schools entails responsibility. To that end, the entire community is accountable for making sure high-performing schools with adequate resources are available for all children.

We often see this sense of ownership of public schools in communities with high concentrations of wealthy and middle-class families. These families often move into communities with school districts that have a reputation for high quality public schools heavily funded by local property taxes, leveraged government subsidies, and private funding. These families elect to pay premium prices for housing in these communities with the expectation that such an investment brings unquestionable entitlement.

The phenomenon of *ownership* is not apparent in urban communities with high concentrations of minority groups. The vast majority of the public in many Black-led school districts have not performed as owners of their local public schools. In spite of their new political standing, the public continues to show behaviors typical of disenfranchisement—sitting on the sidelines of education politics and neither building nor sustaining the important coalitions necessary to demand high-quality, high-performing schools. To understand this phenomenon—the absence of public will in Black-led communities—it was necessary to learn how the public viewed their relationship with the local school district.

What were the causes for this disconnect between the public and the MVSD? Was the public ready to take its place as owners of its local school districts? Specifically, we searched for positive indicators of the public's capacity to take on an ownership role, the public's knowledge of what was taking place in their public schools, and their understanding of the public's role as owners of public education. With this information, the next step would be to explore their perceptions of what barriers would have to be overcome to sustain an educational coalition over time.

Who Owns Mount Vernon Public Schools?

To understand the extent to which respondents embraced the notion of public ownership of public schools, and to gauge the extent to which the public in Mount Vernon understood it had a legitimate claim to ownership of its public schools, the first step was to ask respondents the following question: "Who owns public schools in Mount Vernon?" Respondents were not constrained by the number of options they could select. Six categories emerged that reflected the range of initial responses given by interviewees. As shown in Table 12.1, they include: (1) the public (2) the school board trustees (3) the superintendent (4) the government (5) only parents with children in the school district, and (6) other, which included specific names of political organizations in the community, such as the Black United Clergy or the Italian Civic Association.

Although 50 percent of respondents identified the public as owners, it became clear during the course of analysis that respondents had a variety of ways of interpreting this question. Some answered the question from the factual perspective of who owned public schools. Other respondents answered the question from a normative perspective of who should own public schools. Recognizing that their responses were based on two alternative interpretations, the data were re-analyzed and these new categories were generated to more precisely document who the public believed owns public schools.

Table 12.1
Responses to the Question: "Who Owns the Public Schools?" (Initial Analysis)

Owner	**Stakeholder Group** Specialist	CBO	CAL	Influentials	Total
Public	15 %	18 %	7 %	11 %	51 %
School Board Trustees	4 %	7 %	4 %	3 %	18 %
Superintendent	3 %	3 %	3 %	0 %	9 %
Government	1 %	1 %	8 %	0 %	10 %
Parents of Students	1 %	1 %	1 %	3 %	6 %
Other	5 %	0 %	0 %	1 %	6 %
Total	29 %	30 %	23 %	18 %	100 %

- *The public definitely does not own public schools*. Responses assigned to this code were from respondents whose initial answer was something other than the *public owned public schools*. But after a thorough discussion, they held to their initial response that an entity other than the public owned public schools.

- *Although in theory the public may own public schools, public ownership in Mount Vernon is not a reality*. Responses assigned to this code were respondents whose initial answer was something other than the public. But after discussion, they clarified their answer to mean that, while they believed the public ought to own public schools, this is not the case in Mount Vernon.

- *The public definitely owns but does not exercise its ownership*. Responses assigned to this code were respondents who initially answered "the public," but after discussion, clarified their answer to mean that, while the public owns public education, in Mount Vernon the public has not claimed ownership.

- *Tentatively, the public owns.* Responses assigned to this code were respondents who answered something other than public initially, and after some discussion, exhibited a lack of understanding of public ownership, based on the principles of democracy. They were, however, willing to agree that the public may own public education, but not to embrace the definition as one they could personally adopt.

- *Public definitely owns public school.* Responses assigned to this code were respondents who understood that the public owned public schools, based on the principles of democracy, whether or not they took responsibility for it.

Results of the re-analysis of responses based on these five categories are shown in Table 12.2.

Table 12.2
Responses to the Question: "Who Owns the Public Schools?" (Re-Analysis)

Post	**Stakeholder Group**				
Discussion Response	**Specialist**	**CBO**	**CAL**	**Influentials**	**Total**
Public definitely does not own	3 %	4 %	5 %	1 %	13 %
Public owns in theory; other entity owns	14 %	8 %	11 %	4 %	37 %
Public owns; does not exercise ownership	9 %	8 %	3 %	4 %	24 %
Tentatively, public owns	1 %	3 %	1 %	1 %	6 %
Public definitely owns	3 %	7 %	3 %	7 %	20 %
Total	30 %	30 %	23 %	17 %	100 %

The Public Owns Public Schools

Based on the re-analysis, the responses took a very different direction. As opposed to 50 percent of respondents who identified the public as owners of public education, as shown in Table 12.1, the revised categories revealed that only 18 percent of respondents recognized the public as owners of public education based on principles of democracy, as shown in Table 12.2. Although respondents who recognized the public as owners of public schools were at one end of the pendulum, they represented a core group of people who made no apology for owning and taking responsibility for public education.

These respondents suggested that the problem was rooted in the fact that so few people are willing to acknowledge ownership. They described how residents were displeased with the state of public education, but their displeasure was imbedded in a sense of apathy and not in a desire to do anything about this problem. In essence, it does not affect them personally, so why bother? One respondent used an analogy about tigers and lions to convey his sense of the apathy on the part of the public in Mount Vernon:

> I was reading something today. . . . He was talking about tigers and lions and I know about tigers and lions. And basically what he said was that a tiger would never attack a lion in the presence of another lion, because lions will fight as a matter of pride. Whereas a lion can attack a tiger in the midst of other tigers, and as long as the other tigers are not being threatened, they will not get involved. They will not get involved. And so the writer said that, theoretically, a lion, if he had the means and capability, could destroy a whole pride of tigers. Of course, he'd need to have the strength and the stamina, because he would have to fight them one by one. Because, they'd just sit there and just wait for them. And I think a lot of times in Mount Vernon we're like tigers. In that sense we don't [get] involved because it doesn't affect us. And I don't think that's right.

This respondent went on to describe the importance of being involved. He, along with other respondents, understood that he was doing an injustice to his own children by not fighting for quality education for all children. They recognized the responsibility of holding public officials accountable. Once they elect their leaders, people become complacent, trusting the professionals to work on their behalf. An education specialist described how people, especially in the Black community, tend to put too much confidence in their elected officials:

> I think when people feel that they have people, qualified people, in certain positions, they tend to just allow it to be and not remain involved. And I think that's what you have here right now. You have

> basically nobody watching the henhouse, cuz they're assuming that everything is gonna be all right, because of the fact that African Americans predominate the school board. But as a parent, and as a community member, and as a taxpayer in the city of Mount Vernon, you have got to watch the henhouse.

This group of respondents was passionate about public education, the role of the public in it, and the responsibility that went with ownership.

The Public is Not the Owner of Public Schools

On the other end of the pendulum were those respondents whose comments suggested that they either had no clue about who owned public schools or that there were conditions under which public ownership could be forfeited. They represented 32 percent of all respondents. A college student who had recently graduated from Mount Vernon High School participated in the study. The following statement provides insight into the level of unawareness on the part of some respondents regarding public ownership of public schools:

> Who owns them? I really have no idea. The government? The—I don't know.
>
> Researcher: Well, what about the people in the community, do they own it?
>
> Well, they play a part in it because I figure their tax money goes to education, but do they own it? I don't know.
>
> Researcher: You think the government owns it?
>
> That's what I would think, but then I'm like along with that the people's money does go into that 'cause I know there's always been such a debate about. So, okay, taxes are higher and there's budget cuts and this and that. So I guess the people do play a part, but I don't know if they're completely responsible.
>
> Researcher: Well, who runs the buildings?
>
> That's true. So wait, do you know the answer? Are you going to tell me? No?

Parents from other countries processed the concept of ownership in the following way:

> I think that's why the City Council is in place. Not the City Council. The Board of Ed. From the superintendent to the board members, they would have to advocate, and make sure that the city gets what they need.
>
> Researcher: Well, dating back to colonial days, the public owned public schools.
>
> That's what they say. I learned that in PTA that the public belongs, owns the public schools. But—there's so many blocks, that the public does not even have access to, that would not allow them to even make that statement a true statement. I mean, it's fine; it sounds wonderful, that the public owns the public schools. But in all re—realistically? I don't think so. 'Cause if the public owned the public schools, then the public should have the options of dictating to administration and the state, if they had to go to that level, what is necessary for their children's growth in the education system. How—what is necessary? What tools do we really need? And make sure that those tools are there for our children. I don't think the public even realizes that they own the public schools! I wasn't even knowing that the public owns the public schools!
>
> Researcher: Do you think Scarsdale will feel the same way?
>
> Heck, no! They get what they need!

Public Ownership is Conditional

Some respondents believed there were conditions under which the public could claim ownership. One high-ranking government official believed that if the public did not vote, they did not own the institution; and if people were elected under those conditions, elected officials were not accountable to the public. For example, given the low turnout of the most recent election, trustees who won seats on the board would not be accountable to the public. Other leaders felt the same way. In those instances, the public forfeited their right to ownership.

One respondent, a leading religious figure, added another dimension to this sense of forfeiture of ownership. He believed that the public owned public schools, but explained that once they elected their representatives, public ownership was revoked:

> The trustees own it. Because they make the decisions on who will be hired, they set the public policies. They set the policies for the schools, they have the capacity to evaluate it, they define the budget, they decide what's going to be built and what's not going to be built. Nobody else owns it like that. Nobody else has the ownership. They have—the trustees have the ownership, even though they are put there by the public. Once they are there, they own the schools. . . . The role of the public is they select the trustees, but once selected, the public delegates their authority to the trustees. They give it up, that's what it means to elect them. They give it up.

To advance the conversation, the researcher defined the concept of ownership as a function of democracy. This respondent was steadfast in his response and reflected the attitudes of respondents who believed that public ownership of public schools was conditional and that it could be forfeited:

> I don't see the trustees as individuals—I see them as an entity. They participate in the entity that owns the schools. And the public decides who's going to participate in that entity. To the degree that the public makes the selection, they own it. But they own it only to give it up. That's what we do with public: We give it up to somebody else.

Although this group represented only 14 percent of respondents, they suggested that there are segments of the general population who support this viewpoint, including high-ranking leaders involved in shaping the debate for public education.

Public Ownership has Eluded the Public

A majority of respondents, 61 percent, acknowledged that the public held some level of ownership, either real or in theory. When asked, "Does the community own public schools," this respondent replied:

> I doubt it. I doubt it. . . . It should belong to the people who pay for it, but it doesn't. So that's what I'm trying to say. It's not that, when you have a board, they say no, this is what we're going to do. That goes the other way around.

This group felt that somehow public ownership of public schools was not within the reach of the people of Mount Vernon. It had either been usurped, or it had been voluntarily relinquished by the public. Among those respondents who suggested that public ownership had been usurped or stolen, 18 percent believed it had been usurped by the board of trustees. A representative from the business community captured the sentiments of those who shared this view:

> It should be the citizens of the City of Mount Vernon. However, I think to a large degree that we've allowed the school board to make that their own little fiefdom, which is not good. But that's what happens when people get frustrated: they just throw up their hands after a while and say, 'Okay, fine. You want it? Take it. I'll go somewhere else.' And unfortunately, there's a whole group of parents and children that have no alternative. And they not only get frustrated but they're usually the parents that can't articulate what the problems are, what their issues are, even what their concerns are; and there's nowhere for them to go. I'm hoping that at some point, it comes back to the citizens.

Although much of the criticism was aimed at the Board of Education, 11 percent of respondents suggested that government usurped public ownership; 8 percent identified the superintendent; 7 percent identified those who limit ownership to parents and children in the district; and 7 percent identified powerful political entities like the United Black Clergy (UBC) or the ICA.

At the same time, there was a sense of abdication of responsibility on the part of the public. According to one respondent, people had surrendered to apathy, a manifestation of hopelessness:

> I don't see that we really have that much ownership. And maybe that's the problem. Maybe everyone is saying, 'Eh, it's the school board, you know, it's the school district, we can't do anything about it.'
>
> Researcher: Some would say schools belong to the taxpayers.
>
> Yeah, but we've abdicated that responsibility to these people who don't seem to have the same values. But then again, maybe that situation's all right [with] most people. I don't know. I have the same criticism of the city. I walk down Gramatan Avenue and I'm like, 'How is this acceptable? What planet am I from that this offends me so?' But every-

> one else seems to not—it's almost like they don't see it. Like if you're assaulted enough, you just don't feel it anymore, you don't see it. Visual assault, you just don't see it.

Responses to the question of public ownership suggest that lack of public involvement is complex. It is not simply the fact of people not caring or their prioritizing other issues over involvement in education. Many of the people in Mount Vernon care deeply about public education. They are angry, frustrated, and disillusioned with their leaders. Some also felt victimized by having had a fundamental right stolen from them.

Chapter 13

Building Public Support for Public Schools

Given the insights into the state of the public and its relationship with the MVSD provided by the interview process, the next step was to explore the extent to which respondents would be willing to work with fellow residents to build public support for public education. The political climate within the education landscape was intense, with more than 60 percent of interview respondents believing that public schools were no longer theirs. In addition, a large segment of the population was disenfranchised. Those who were engaged were disgruntled with the district, angry with the leaders of the clergy, and suspicious of everyone who might be involved in education policy. Under these conditions, were there common elements around which this public might unite in support of higher-achieving schools?

Building a Coalition of Support for Public Schools

Only a small contingent, 8 percent, did not support building a coalition in support of public schools, as shown in Table 13.1. Among the stakeholder groups, education specialists were the most skeptical.

One building leader provided insight into how difficult it might be to change the mindset of education professionals. This building leader explained the difficulty of building a coalition in support of public schools in this way:

> What if they do that? I just think of one more organization where people talk, talk, complain, complain, and do nothing, nothing, nothing.

Researcher: So you think there would be no value?

If it's not productive, it's a waste of time. I'm not saying that that particular thing that you're talking about would be the case, but I'd be a little leery about it at first, because it seems to be that everybody is an expert at when it comes to education, everybody is an expert, or they think what it should be. And—but they're not there. They're not in the trenches and they don't know. I don't know, I get a little leery of that.

Table 13.1
Responses to Question: "Do You Favor Building a Coalition in Support of Public Education?"

	Stakeholder Group				
Supports Coalition	**Specialist**	**CBO**	**CAL**	**Influentials**	**Total**
Yes	19 %	23 %	21 %	12 %	75 %
Tentative Yes	7 %	5 %	1 %	5 %	18 %
No, would be a waste of time	4 %	1 %	1 %	1 %	7 %
Total	30 %	29 %	23 %	18 %	100 %

Some educators who thought it would be a good idea discussed the challenge of changing attitudes about the public's being the legitimate owners of public education. To make this point, one school official described how parents are not given the respect they are due and how educators tend to work only with parents they can control:

One of the things I find when working with parents is that parents genuinely know what their children need. And sometimes educators take that for granted, you know, and think that we know it all, because we have the PhD and the Master's. But sometimes it's shadowed by personal—people with hidden agendas. Sometimes, we purposely select who we want to be involved—those who don't give us a hard time. Those who don't hassle too much, the ones we can manipulate are the ones we want. —But I think, I think, yeah, that has been my experience.

Educators were not alone in expressing reservations. A single male parent who spends a great deal of his time doing volunteer services for children in the community had similar misgivings. He did not feel a coalition could work in Mount Vernon, because "Personal agendas of individuals always override what is in the best interest for children." Based on his experience as a volunteer, he went on to describe the frustrations of working with people who get involved for the wrong reasons:

> And, usually, when people get involved with this, you have that handful of people who have left their ego at the door, but the people who end up leading it are the people with the biggest egos. But, unfortunately, somehow it's human behavior. Those egos kick in and then what happens is everyone loses sight of what they were there for.

Despite these reservations, the vast majority, 73 percent of respondents across all stakeholder groups, believed building a coalition was a great idea. People felt it would be a good vehicle for demanding accountability as well as for being held accountable. Undergirding much of the discussion on this issue was a sense that a coalition would take education out of the political quagmire in which it currently operates. People suggested that the education landscape in Mount Vernon has always been the embodiment of a contentious mindset. A coalition that was designed to bring people together would begin the long-overdue process of healing for the city. A Fleetwood resident captured this sentiment:

> Oh, I think that would be a very good thing. I think that has been a stumbling block in this community for a very long time, because it's always been seemingly the 'us' against 'them' and the 'us' sometimes is not necessarily even White, but what is perceived as, uh, even Blacks who have more money. So it's the 'us' against 'them.' Us, who can send our kids to the private or parochial schools versus those who can't. And in some ways, while I think I understand the church leaders' desire to try to build their community up and try to get people to empower themselves, I feel in some ways that has created an 'us' against 'them' kind of mentality as well.

In discussing key issues for building a coalition among education specialists in support of coalition building, respondents identified issues around which this group might rally, as shown in Table 13.2. After much discussion, the top two issues most agreed on were a demand for excellence and parent and community involvement within the district.

Table 13.2
Key Issues for a Coalition to Address as Identified by Education Specialists Supportive of a Coalition

	Education Specialist Stakeholder
Demand for Excellence in Public Education	45 %
Accountability	10 %
Parent / Community Involvement in Education System	20 %
Increased Access to School Facilities/Services	7 %
Safety / Social Order	16 %
Other	2 %
Total	100 %

Overcoming Barriers to Coalition Building

In spite of the high level of enthusiasm around building a coalition, respondents were not naive in their recognition of how difficult it would be to build an enduring organization. A recurring refrain among those who responded was that the citizens of Mount Vernon were their own worst enemies. They suggested that the greatest strength the people possessed—diversity—was the very factor that frustrated their potential for unity. Bias, discrimination, fear, and a basic disrespect for difference was identified by 37 percent as the number one barrier that would have to be overcome. The lack of tolerance for differences in ethnicity among factions of the new majority, long-held biased views about the old majority, and overall ideological differences were described as impediments to building a unified coalition. Second to intolerance were personal agendas, big egos, and a lack of cooperative spirit, cited by 27 percent of respondents.

Of the major assets for building their ideal schools and getting things done, the two most often cited were the city's small town characteristics and its citizens' propensity to care about one another. Everybody knows almost everybody else and people have built relationships over the years from which they can draw political capital. At the same time, these relationships, along with the small town nature of the city, have led to perceptions of people operating within their own political factions, using their affiliations for their own political agenda, their organization's political agenda, or both. Some respondents complained that people have become self-serving, using the educational system as a stepping stone to higher levels of power.

An Independent Organization with Full Support of Stakeholders

In exploring the type of organizational structure respondents envisioned for a coalition in support of public schools, there was strong sentiment that such a coalition should have an independent base of operations. As a result, financial independence would be among the criteria viewed as essential for a sustainable organization. It would also need to have the full support of important stakeholders, including representatives from the highest level of government, the office of the superintendent, and the business community. Also critical would be the collective representation of an interdenominational religious community, including nontraditional denominations important to select ethnic groups. Respondents also believed that the organization must include members of the community that have traditionally been excluded from the conversation. For example, 50 percent of respondents stressed the importance of including emerging underrepresented minority groups, such as residents from the Brazilian community. Another 25 percent identified the youth and the elderly, while 16 percent identified people who have no direct relationship with the district, and 9 percent identified other groups.

Respondents had definite thoughts on who should lead the coalition and around what issues the coalition should rally. In many ways, respondents felt that the most difficult challenge would be to develop a process for selecting the group's leader. Given the nature of Mount Vernon politics, a group that might be perceived as the wrong combination of stakeholders could also sabotage any attempt for a citywide coalition. The process for selection would have to stand the test of public scrutiny.

Table 13.3
Potential Sources of Group or Individual Leaders for a Coalition

Potential Coalition Leader	Stakeholder Group Specialist	CBO	CAL	Influentials	Total
Educator	2 %	2 %	2 %	2 %	8 %
School District Representatives	0 %	5 %	0 %	2 %	7 %
CBO	4 %	6 %	2 %	2 %	14 %
Churches/Clergy	7 %	4 %	4 %	0 %	15 %
Government Representatives	4 %	2 %	2 %	2 %	10 %
Parents/Community Members	14 %	11 %	15 %	6 %	46 %
Other	0 %	0 %	0 %	0 %	0 %
Total	31 %	30 %	25 %	14 %	100 %

The leader would have to be an individual who was perceived by the public as a genuine advocate for children. As shown in Table 13.3, almost half—48 percent—of respondents across all stakeholder groups, indicated that the leader should emerge from the ranks of the public, perhaps a parent or a member of the at-large community.

Part Four

Voices from Focus Groups

Chapter 14

The Community Focus Groups

Three community focus groups were conducted in August 2007 with people who resided in or who heavily identified with one of three distinct neighborhoods within Mount Vernon: the south side; the north side; and the Fleetwood section. The south side focus group was held at a participant's apartment at Levister Towers, a subsidized housing complex that currently houses low- and moderate-income families. It was made up of six women who were college-educated, POAD, and single. Three of the respondents were employed by the MVSD. One had two children who attended public school in the district; another had a child who was not yet of school age.

The north side focus group was held at the home of a participant. It comprised six women who were POAD and who worked in the human services field or in the community. Five were college-educated. One was a former education administrator and two were elementary school teachers.

The Fleetwood focus group was held at the home of a participant who was the third generation to live in her home. Its members, five women and one man, had had various experience in business and in community participation; all were White. One woman worked as a teaching assistant for the MVSD and had children attending public school in the district.

Community focus group respondents were asked the same questions as in-depth interview respondents. A cross-analysis of data among the community focus groups revealed a high level of congruence with interview data. Drawing from these two different sources helps reduce potential bias and offers a higher degree of validity for the findings.

The Importance of Education

On a scale of one to ten (with one being the most important and ten being the least), what importance would you say the people of Mount Vernon would give to public education?

Respondents from each community focus group believed public education was of value to the people of Mount Vernon. Similar to the interview respondents, several community focus group respondents had attended public schools and spoke fondly of their experience. Individual respondents conveyed stories of people who valued education, many of whom spent much of their adult lives working in and attending schools in a variety of settings. For example, most of the participants of the south side group had had some form of college or vocational training and showed an obvious pride in their educational accomplishments. One woman from the north side group talked about her years struggling to achieve a master's degree. A Fleetwood respondent talked fondly of attending an integrated public school and how it shaped his life.

South side participants believed the people would rank education as very important and gave it the highest ranking. The north side participants believed the public would rank education as important and assigned it a number two. The Fleetwood participants gave the ranking question a four to five ranking, indicating that the public would rank public education as somewhat important. These responses were consistent with responses from participants in the in-depth interviews.

There was also quite a bit of discussion among the south side group about why people do not vote. Reasons ranged from a lack of information for making an informed decision to an absence of a family tradition of voting. The greatest cause, however, was apathy. One community respondent offered the following view:

> All right, so voting, it's like it has to be—it's something—you're going to vote if you see your parents voting. If you saw your grandmother voting, your mother, your father. You're going to vote. Hey, I'm going to vote, too, because it's a family tradition or whatever you want to call it. It's passed down. But if your family isn't used to, if you're not used to seeing your family voting, then you're not going to go out and vote either. A lot of Black people don't vote. Their grandparents didn't vote. Their mother didn't vote. Their father didn't vote, and I don't vote. I'm not trying to be funny.
>
> Researcher: Why don't you vote?

> I don't vote because sometimes I feel like especially for the—I don't want to get off track—but I don't vote because I feel sometimes that it just won't make a difference. That one vote might be the one that might carry me over, but I just feel like sometimes they're going to do what they want to do anyway. They're going put in who they want to put in anyway. They're not going to listen to little old me. Which may not be true, but that's how I think sometimes. And that's the honest truth.

South side respondents believed public education to be very important to the people of Mount Vernon, but saw no correlation between how those people feel about education and what they do to demonstrate its importance. One respondent understood why people did not vote and admitted that she had voted for the first time at the age of thirty, although education has always been important to her. North side participants had similar feelings; however, they were not sympathetic to people who do not vote. These responses were consistent with responses we received from in-depth interviews.

Fleetwood residents did not believe education was very important to the people of Mount Vernon, and talked quite a bit about other priorities, such as lower taxes and quality-of-life issues. They believed education is not as important to the public as public safety. They also affirmed perceptions of bright flight taking place within the district. Participants acknowledged the presence of a bedroom community that had no interest in public schools, especially in Mount Vernon. Several members in the Fleetwood group described their personal decisions not to send their children to school in the district after elementary school or how they moved to Mount Vernon in spite of the public schools.

Respondents from the three community focus groups confirmed several findings also found in the in-depth interviews. First, a great deal of apathy exists among the voting population. Second, there are many families who choose alternative educational settings for their children. Third, a leading cause of bright flight is the issue of crime and disorder in the middle and high schools.

The Ideal School

Describe the ideal school you envision for the children of Mount Vernon.

Participants in all three community focus groups had a clear sense of what they envisioned for the education of Mount Vernon's children. They identified components of their ideal school that were similar to those of interview respondents. Technology, dedicated teachers, open and diverse curricula, small learning environments, and modern physical plants were among the key components they wanted for their ideal school. Participants across the community focus groups did not place as much emphasis on safety and order as a component in their ideal school. However, one participant from the south side group talked about the need for more "quiet" in schools, which was interpreted to mean a more orderly, less chaotic school environment. A Fleetwood respondent said that an ideal school would teach students how to become critical thinkers.

A respondent who had a child in the system raised concerns about the No Child Left Behind (NCLB) program and its overemphasis on test taking. This respondent described how it was not something she wanted for her ideal school:

> I think a school that doesn't just teach the kids facts, it teaches the kids how to learn. One thing that I got from Bronxville was a lot of headaches, but a lot of, umm, knowledge of how to find the information I need. Not necessarily actual facts, but how to find out the facts and think for myself.

In the context of the ideal-school discussion, the respondent also confirmed concerns about performance issues at the elementary school level that were also expressed by interview respondents.

Preparing Students for the Future

Is Mount Vernon preparing its youth for their future?

The range of responses given by the community focus group participants to this question was somewhat consistent with responses collected from interview respondents. Overall, respondents across all three community focus groups did not feel Mount Vernon was preparing its youth for the future. They discussed how the district schools had changed over the years. After-school programs, Boy Scouts and Girl Scouts, dance, and arts and crafts were among the things respondents missed from public schools. South side respondents talked about the absence of order in the schools. They described how order and respect for others were not as apparent in the district today.

North side respondents were not as forthcoming in their views about public schools. Several had no children in the district or had not been involved for years. Their overall perception, however, was that the children were not being prepared for the future. One of the educators in the group was very vocal and talked about how elementary school students are not as prepared as most seem to feel. Although the elementary schools are receiving national recognition, she strongly believed the students lacked the critical skills needed for middle school academic rigor. She described the district's inability to process so many children with special needs and English Language (ELA) classifications. She also talked about the tremendous number of students coming from the Bronx, who enter the system with academic deficiencies.

Respondents from Fleetwood concurred with much of what was discussed concerning the district's inadequacies in both the middle and elementary schools. A parent whose child attended one of the north side's blue ribbon schools spoke about how even in those schools, children are not prepared. Her response to the question, "Is the district preparing its youth for their future?" was as follows:

> No, they're not. They can pass a test. By the time those kids get to sixth grade, they have spent fourth grade preparing for three separate tests. Third grade preparing for two tests. Fourth grade is a wash-out. Fourth grade is useless except for getting ready for a test. Fifth grade, now they're two years behind because all of the things they should have been learning in science, in social studies, in all of that, they haven't been learning because there's no test in that so it doesn't matter. By sixth grade, these kids are now another two years behind because there's two more tests in fifth grade: the social studies test, which they cram for the first month and a half of school, and a science test. So by sixth grade, these kids go in and don't know what apostrophes are used for. They don't know where to put a comma in a list. They don't know any of the basics. They don't know how to do a bibliography. Most kids go through elementary and then, because of the implication of the high school environment, they're taking their kids out and sending them to private school after elementary.

Community focus group participants were more critical of school performance issues than interview respondents. No respondent from any of the community focus groups gave the district either a good or mixed review on the district's performance, while 16 percent of interview respondents gave the district a good rating and 28 percent gave the school a mixed rating. These differences may be attributed to the differences in knowledge about the system between interview and community focus group participants. The north side focus group had a few educators within their group who felt that standardized test scores were not the only indicator to measure success and pointed to other instruments to make judgments about school performance. They were all neighbors and appeared comfortable to discuss the topic openly. Participants of the Fleetwood group were also very candid with their remarks. One parent, in particular, was comfortable with describing why elementary school children were not being prepared for their future. She was a parent who worked in the classroom as a teaching assistant within the district and was an active member of the PTA. In addition, the Fleetwood group was comprised of officers of the neighborhood association, who appeared to be a more informed citizenry.

The Two Most Critical Problems

What are the two most critical problems facing the Mount Vernon School District?

Each of the community focus groups was instructed to discuss this question and come to a consensus on their two responses. South side respondents identified violence and the absence of a strong curriculum as the first and second most critical problems. Lack of leadership was heavily debated, but ultimately eliminated as one of their selections. The north side group chose lack of leadership and lack of parent involvement as the first and second most critical problems. The Fleetwood group selected the absence of safety in the schools as the most critical problem facing the district and cited lack of leadership as the second.

Responses from focus group participants substantiate the findings of the interviews. Almost 42 percent of interview respondents identified the absence of school safety and order as the first major problem facing the district, and 24 percent of identified the absence of leadership as the second.

Similar to several discussions held during the in-depth interviews, these conversations about leadership took on a very speculative tone. People were not sure what was happening, but their intuition attributed it to a lack of leadership at the level of the board. According to one Fleetwood respondent, "Leadership is at the top. I don't know how the board is structured, but, yes. Yeah, I don't think you would be putting words in my mouth. There is something that seems to be fundamentally amiss."

A lengthy discussion ensued that pointed to problems at the board level. The following captures the essence of their discussion:

> Respondent 1: I don't think you have a good board.
>
> Respondent 2: If you get a good board, those things happen.
>
> Respondent 1: Teachers come to school with a curriculum. They know how to teach.
>
> Respondent 2: That's right.
>
> Respondent 1: If no one tells them what to do, they can still be good teachers. Probably better teachers.
>
> Respondent 2: And if we have a better board, the curriculum will fall into place.

How Things Get Done

How do things get done for public education in Mount Vernon?

South side participants believed that things get done behind closed doors and that this is not a good thing for the public. The following remark summarized the feeling of the group:

> . . . and that's why people don't get involved, because we figure that things are all covered up and it's just certain people that got say-so and—uh—so, because I even go to the board meetings sometimes and it's just like that. It's just like that. It's just like what you gotta say is not going to matter anyway, but you can go. But it's just like that. Things don't get done and everything is done behind closed doors.

Three respondents from the Fleetwood group chose to not participate in the discussion, because of their lack of awareness of the process. However, those who participated agreed that things got done behind closed doors. North side respondents believed that things got done through a combination of a formal process and behind closed doors. A long discussion took place among north side respondents about the effects of a closed process.

Both interview and community focus group participants expressed little faith in the processes used to get things done for education. An estimated 79 percent of interview respondents believed decisions are made either through a combination of a formal process and behind closed doors, or just behind closed doors. Similar to perceptions of interview respondents, community focus groups alluded to the formal process as being just a facade for decisions that already have been made. In their perception, such decisions are sometimes not in the best interest of children. One north side participant summed up the essence of the conversation as follows:

> No, it's not a good thing and here's why: because the school district is a public institution and if decisions are being made behind closed doors, and the public is not privy to them, then the public has no input in it and I think that's a bad thing. We know who's going to be the next principal. We know who's getting bumped and someone's assistant is getting—I mean, those deals are made behind. I know people that have been interviewed when they already know who they're going to pick, and I guess that happens everywhere. The problem is that might not be the best person for the job. See, it just has a domino effect, because then you have teachers who cannot teach, administrators who cannot administrate, and then that starts. It eventually trickles down to the children and then they don't achieve, because the people cannot do the job.

These, as well as remarks from the other focus groups substantiate the findings from the in-depth interviews.

Getting Along

What is the relationship between the public and its school district?

The community focus groups' responses to this question were consistent with responses from interviews in which 31 percent of interview respondents who stated that their personal relationship, or their organization's relationship with the district, was good or improving. South side respondents spoke of the good relationships that had been developed over the years with their children's teachers and principals. North side participants spoke of a working relationship that had improved over the years. The Fleetwood group spoke with pride about their scholarship programs and other efforts they have made to help the MVSD.

Although Fleetwood respondents felt their relationship with the district was good, they made the point that the relationship was not reciprocal. One participant described it the following way: "Sounds like we have a relationship that, when we offer something to the school, they take it, but there is no reciprocal relationship or dialogue."

Every individual who took part in a community focus group felt the relationship between the public and the board was not very good. A south side respondent described a process that was too cumbersome for public involvement. One described a board that was untrustworthy:

> That's the thing, you've always got to wait because they speak with a forked tongue. The outcome is always just the opposite. But for the school board, I know that you can go up to the school board, which is great, and a lot of people are very excited. They go to the school board meetings wanting to voice their opinions and wanting to be heard. They get up there and they give you that little time and they say, 'Thank you for coming.' You have a seat and you think you made a difference only to find out later that what you said, and what other people said, parents and concerned members of the community, and the reality is that you just did what you did but no real major impact was made based on the forum at hand. It's like that all of the time. I know a lot of people don't even really like going to the board meetings. I remember, at one time, the board room would be filled. Standing room only. It's over.

One north side participant described the relationship as one of "outraged dissolution, absolute disillusionment, total disconnection." This north side participant expressed the sense of disconnection within the community: "I've been out petitioning and they say 'what's the use of voting?' The people get in there and say one thing and then change their minds." This respondent went on to say that this disconnectedness is a result of a lack of parent involvement, lack of leadership, and a lack of a curriculum to prepare young children to be critical-thinking adults.

Community Perceptions of Ownership

Who owns public schools?

This question evoked a lively discussion among participants in each of the community focus groups, as it did with interview respondents. Some focus group participants did not know that the public owned the public schools or that they were part of that public. Some thought that an entity other than the public owned public schools. Some felt that although the public might own public schools in actuality or in theory, as far as they were concerned, public ownership of schools in Mount Vernon had been somehow forfeited or stolen.

Most responses of the south side focus group participants were similar to responses of most interview respondents who were unaware that the public owned the public schools and who were unaware that they were part of that public. Among interview respondents, there was a strong lack of awareness regarding the public's ownership of public schools, as only 9 percent recognized ownership of public schools as a function of their democracy. South side focus group participants held similar perceptions, although participants in the south side focus group believed that the government owns public schools. In response to the question about who owns public schools, one member from the south side group responded after a long silence as follows:

> Respondent 1: The public. We are C'mon guys.
>
> Respondent 2: She said it. That's funny.
>
> Respondent 1: I agree that's the way it should be, but—
>
> Respondent 3: But the state runs the public school.
>
> Respondent 2: Right.
>
> Respondent 3: That's the way it should be, but the people don't own the public school. Well, they should own it. They're paying the taxes and—
>
> Respondent 1: Hold on, hold on. Hold on. Who owns the public schools? They're public, so the public owns the public schools. But we don't act like we own it. So, maybe we need to do our job.
>
> Respondent 4: It's funny, because if you get that one parent that comes to school and makes that big deal and be like "I'm paying your salary," everybody looks at her like she's crazy. But it's true.
>
> Respondent 3: So, if we own the public schools, the public, then why is there so much chaos? How come things aren't going right?
>
> Respondent 2: Why does the state have to take over if the public owns—okay. That's a good question. You know why? Because the public don't know that they own the public school. I didn't know that.

Researcher: You didn't know that?

Respondent 2: No, I thought the state. I thought the state, because they always have to come in and—

Respondent 3: We don't know we own it.

Researcher: Who owns the state?

Respondent 2: The State?

Respondent 4: The Federal Government.

Researcher: Who owns the federal government?

Respondent 2: I want you to tell me!

Respondent 1: I don't have the slightest idea.

Respondent 4: We own this country. That's it. And everything that we do and that's why it's important for us to vote because we put people in places to make these decisions based for us. When we don't vote, they do what they want to do and if you put the wrong person in a seat, and sometimes when you vote, you put the wrong person in a seat anyways.

The Fleetwood focus group held a lively debate over whether schools were owned by the City Council, the US Congress, the State of New York, or the Board of Education. Like the typical interview respondents, most in the Fleetwood group agreed that, at least in theory, the public owned public schools; but in Mount Vernon, they thought public schools were owned by some branch of government. The following presents a brief exchange that reflects how the question was processed by a participant in the Fleetwood group. It opens with a respondent answering the question, "Who owns public schools?"

Respondent 1: The constituents. You're trying to be cute.

Researcher: I'm not trying to be cute.

Respondent 1: The citizens. Of course. So it all devolves back to the citizen. That's why I asked you what you meant by the word ownership.

Respondent 2: I think that's a philosophical notion.

Respondent 1: Well, that's why I asked her what she means by ownership.

Respondent 2: Well, ownership, I agree with that.

Researcher: You pay taxes?

Respondent 1: Yeah.

Researcher: You decide on the taxes, too.

Respondent 1: I guess it's a semantic . . .

Respondent 3, interrupting: The mayor reports to us, essentially.

Researcher: You own public schools!

Respondent 3: So does the board.

The group took on an aura of skepticism, in which respondents acknowledged that the public owned public schools in theory, but that in Mount Vernon they really belonged to the government or the Board of Education. After sitting silent through the debate, one respondent offered the following analogy:

> Well, if you want to go with little stories like that, I'll tell you one from the newspaper a few weeks ago, which is not about the Board of Ed., but which relates. A gentleman walked up and said something to Dick Cheney about how he didn't like his policies. Oh, I'm sorry, my mistake. It was Karl Rove and it was that singer walked up. And Karl Rove said, "I don't work for you. I work for the people." And she says, "Well, I am the people." And I guess I thought of Dick Cheney because somebody said something to him and, ten minutes later, [that person] was arrested! [Laughter]

This tone of sarcasm around who really owns public schools was also consistent with responses among interview participants.

North side focus group participants were very aware that public schools belonged to the public, but they made reference to how the Board of Education acted as if it owned public schools. They also discussed the

Black Church and the role it had played in inhibiting the public from feeling a sense of ownership of its public schools, instead of enabling the parishioners to become critical thinkers. Some also felt that some ministers used their influence to gain support for school board candidates who were endorsed by individual members of the clergy. One respondent pointed out that she knew too many people who were unwilling to think for themselves and make up their own minds about school politics:

> I have had too may experiences. I think there are two or three major churches in this area and they get up on their altar or whatever to call it and they tell their congregations how to vote. I have met that over and over again. "Wait, I have to go to church. I have to find out how I'm supposed to vote."

These comments about the recent role of the church were also similar to those of interview participants.

Although several community focus group respondents initially expressed a sense of apathy and believed that little could be done to restore the public to its rightful position of ownership of public schools, discussions among the community focus group participants generated a strong sense of empowerment among participants who came to the realization that they owned public schools. In this regard, the community focus groups demonstrated consistency with 92 percent of interview respondents, who felt that building a coalition of support held value.

This interpretation was substantiated by the spontaneous behavior of one participant. When the discussion about ownership was concluded, a young mother from the south side focus group left the apartment, but returned with two young friends who wanted to know more about the notion of public ownership of public schools. In addition, the young woman who had originally admitted that she did not vote said that she would have to rethink her position.

Finally, the Fleetwood group also demonstrated a sense of empowerment from the knowledge that they owned public schools. By the end of their group discussion, participants talked about the value of people working together for higher-achieving schools.

Chapter 15

The Youth Focus Group

The research for this book grew out of concern over the state of public education in urban America and the tragic loss of so many talented young minority students who are trapped in low-performing, inner-city public schools. A primary aim of this research was to benefit children by exploring meaningful ways for the public to come together in support of higher-achieving schools. In support of this aim, it was important to gather data directly from the intended beneficiaries and to include their voices as an integral part of the data. Thus, a focus group was conducted with youths who, for a variety of reasons, did not succeed in the school system. This focus group was arranged through College Careers, a not-for-profit organization that helps children who have dropped out of school. The group included students enrolled in the College Careers Summer Tutorial Program. Ten students were invited to participate in a focus group after their classes. Three agreed to stay and participate. The meeting was held at the Mount Vernon Public Library in August 2007.

One student was not a resident of Mount Vernon. He was born and raised in Yonkers and attended schools in the Yonkers Public School District until the eleventh grade. He decided to drop out when he realized that in order to meet graduation requirements he would have to stay in school another two years. This young man decided to leave and pursue a GED on his own. His parents are from the Dominican Republic, and he currently resides with them in Yonkers. He has four sisters. He knows a lot of people in Mount Vernon and thought the subject was important enough to participate.

Another student in the College Careers program was a young man who was born and raised in Jamaica, West Indies, and recently moved to

Mount Vernon with his parents. This young man has three sisters and one brother. When he attempted to register for the eleventh grade at the high school, he was advised that he would have to enroll in the ninth grade. Apparently, the decision to assign him to a lower grade was based on administration's assessment of his academic grade level. The young man was not willing to repeat two grades in order to get a high school diploma. He decided to pursue a GED on his own as opposed to enrolling in the MVSD.

The third young man was born and raised in Yonkers and had lived in Mount Vernon for six years. He enrolled in the MVSD in the ninth grade and remained there until he entered the twelfth grade. This young man got arrested at least once and he believes it ultimately resulted in his being forced to drop out of school. He heard about College Careers through friends and family and he desires to obtain a GED. He has one brother and three sisters. Two of his siblings graduated from school and one sister is working on a nursing degree. He feels he is the only one in his family who is "stumbling" in the wrong direction and he wants to "try and do something right." This youngster lives with his mother, who is from Sierra Leone, and a brother. His mother has a nursing degree and works as a registered nurse at a hospital in New York City.

To further substantiate data collected from in-depth interviews, the youth focus group was asked five questions and their responses were compared with responses from the in-depth interviews. These were the questions:

1. If you had to rank the importance of public education to the people of Mount Vernon on a scale of 1 to 10 (with 1 being the most important and 10 being the least important), what ranking would you say the public would give to public education?
2. Can you describe the type of school you would like to attend? What does your ideal school look like?
3. Do you think Mount Vernon is preparing its youth for their future?
4. Is there a role for schools to play in your education that goes beyond just educating you?
5. Can you describe how the public gets along with the people who run the schools?

The Importance of Education

The youths in this focus group believed education was important to the Mount Vernon public. However, they believed the public would rank education at level four or five, i.e., "important" or "somewhat important." They felt education was important to parents and that it was important to parents that their kids did well in school:

> Yeah, it's important to the people. It's important to the parents. But the kids in school, I'm not saying, either private school or government school, but, it's important for the kids to go to school, 'cause, without education, you're nowhere in life. You're just another, you know, brother on the street, doin' what they do.

When asked how they felt about the fact that many parents did not attend parents' meetings or other school events, they said that it did not bother them at all. They understood that parents are busy trying to make ends meet. One young man made the following comment:

> It's probably because the parent that they have is caught up in stuff; is like goin' to work, payin' rent bills. You know, basically tryin' to keep their house goin.' The kid is older now, more mature, can probably take care of himself.

Another student felt that meetings were held during times when parents have to work, making it difficult for them to come to school for fear of losing their jobs.

Two students described why they thought parents did not like coming to the school. They felt teachers spend a lot of time conveying to parents the things their children were doing wrong; that teachers never have anything positive to say about the students; and that teachers never have solutions for how the students can improve. These young men did not believe that parents were willing to take time to go to school to hear nothing but complaints:

> It doesn't affect me, because, every meeting, every year, it all [talk about] the same thing. Which is the conduct, rules and regulations, how your kid should act, what your kids need to continue school, you know, who's the guidance counselor, who's this, who's that, basically the same thing, and, parents don't wanna hear that every year. Every

> month. Every week. They got better things to be doing. I mean, what they wanna hear is, "How's my kid doin'?" "Is he graduatin' to the next class?" "Is his grades up to standards?" Those are the things parents really wanna hear; not come to school, "Your kid is doin' this; your kid is doin' this; your kid's bad; your kid's suspended"—every week, every—who's gonna, degrade the parents for [not] comin' in, you know?
>
> They shouldn't just talk about the negative things. Talk about the positive things, talk about what the school organization's gonna do to improve, the education you know, to get better books and after school activities. Things that the school's gonna do to improve the school. So the school can get an A.

Their responses on the ranking did not completely meet the test for congruence. More than 64 percent of respondents who participated in in-depth interviews ranked education as very important and important. Although the youth focus group participants said education was important to the people, they ranked it slightly lower, as important or somewhat important. Their responses did converge in terms of the parents working very hard on other important priorities.

The Ideal School

Several questions were asked to prompt conversation about their ideal public school: "Tell me what your ideal school would look like. How would it sound? Describe to me somebody in leadership at your ideal school who would really care about kids, about young people." After a long silence, one youth replied, "It's hard to see that type of person." The following represents their collective responses:

> Respondent 1: My ideal school is, uh, it don't have to be enormous, but, nice-size school. Air conditioned, always, work in the summer. New books—not books that have written stuff in it, and ripped sheets and stuff. Teachers who actually care about the students, and not there just to get paid. Females gotta be there. It gotta be a coed school. And principals that care, that are not so worried about what you wearin'. What you got on. Also, a good security system, but somewhere where you can feel safe. You can also know that the teachers, they care about you. They're not just there to make you look bad, or whatever. That's the only way you can learn, you can learn freely.

Maybe TV in some of the rooms, or the lunchrooms. And good lunch, too! Maybe Domino's instead of the school's or something. That's a motivation to keep the kid going to school, if we have McDonald's in the cafeteria—free McDonald's, free lunch. Obviously, the kid's gonna go to school. That show that they actually care about the kids, too. That's my ideal school. If I had that in school, I'd be still in school. I'd be happy to wake up at 7 in the morning, 6:30, go to school.

Respondent 2: I dream that, um, schools system would be less violent. More teachers that care about students, help them with their homework. Class work. And, more educational stuffs.

Researcher: Like?

Respondent 2: Charts. 'Cause there are students who are so—in more social groups? More counsel sessions and things that help you feel better in the school environment. Good recreational program.

The young men's depictions of their ideal school correspond with some of the key elements of an ideal school expressed by respondents who participated in the in-depth interviews: Eighteen percent of interview respondents emphasized the importance of a dedicated teaching staff and almost 14 percent cited a safe environment in which to learn. The youth focus group also described some of the same elements of a school culture conducive to learning that were expressed by 29 percent of interview respondents.

Preparing Students for the Future

The youth focus group believed, to some extent, that the district was preparing them for their future. However, there were instances where they felt they were not being prepared. One young man described many distractions that kept students from learning; for example, disruptive students and teachers who are not teaching to their potential. The statement below expresses his ambivalence about whether Mount Vernon schools were preparing him for his future:

It did. But it didn't at the [same] time. It did, because you go to school, you have to learn something, that day of school that you went to school. You have to pick up. . . . If it's not ten things, you have to pick up at least one thing that you really focus in class about. Like, there's gonna

> be a lot of things pushing your focus away. Once again, violence. Two: probably teacher is not willing to teach at that time. Or, the teacher has some kind of problem with some students in that class, so will kick out the student. You know what happens to the [student] roamin' amongst the hallways, getting into trouble.

Data from the interviews described the difficulty of finding meaningful alternatives to teaching students with behavioral problems. This focus group respondent corroborated that finding with his concerns about distractions in the classroom. Not only did he describe students who are distracted from learning, but also students who misbehave and end up roaming the hallways and are not engaged in another method of learning. Interview respondents spoke about a lack of resolution for this problem and its impact on the learning environment in schools, as did the youth focus group participants.

The Two Most Critical Problems

When the youth focus group was asked to describe the two most critical problems facing the district, one youth described the need for a smaller learning environment and a broader curriculum from which to explore career options. He did not like the idea that Mount Vernon has only one high school. In addition, he felt that the middle schools are too big, too close in proximity, and too crowded. He believed that these factors perpetuate crime and violence in the community. In addition to a smaller learning environment, this youth talked about wanting a diverse curriculum, one which affords students the opportunity to explore different career paths, which he described as follows:

> They should have different classes that teach you different things. So you could really make up the kid's mind, on what they wanna be, in the future, when they're young. But Mount Vernon doesn't have that. It only have [School Name] and [School Name]. And they're right next to each other. So they bound to meet up, after school. And that's how crimes, violence are increased.

Because the issue of crime and violence among youth was a dominant theme throughout the interview process, the researcher took the opportunity to query the youth focus group for their perspectives on how it could be eliminated. One student immediately replied, "First, you should separate the schools; two, put police, put more security in the schools. Put more police enforcement outside." The youth were asked what they believed could be done to completely eliminate crime. All three of the focus group respondents agreed that nothing can be done and that it is just the way of life: "You can't eliminate violence, violence comes regardless of what you say or what you do, violence is going to come."

One young man said that ways in which students are treated at school may contribute to the perpetuation of crime. His remarks confirm what many described as the importance of teachers in the life of students, especially troubled students. He described how behaviors brought on by teachers can perpetuate crime and why crime, to him, is such a fact of life:

> You can't get to that point no matter where you at, because if you think about it, you know, if you're in class and the teacher kicks you out of class, how is that kid mentality going to be? He's going to have some kind of feelings for the teacher. And every day he or she comes to class, the teacher kicks he or she out of the class, it's going to build up the animosity that the kid, or he or she, has towards the teacher. To the point that he or she either stabs the teacher, or brings a gun into the school, shoot everybody up. You can't really eliminate the violence; it all depends on the staff. If the staff do what they're supposed to do, teach how they're supposed to teach, I mean, be friendly towards the students, stuff like this wouldn't happen. It's basically about the staff.
>
> Researcher: So you think we could begin eliminating violence by the staff treating students differently.
>
> Yeah, because, believe me, I've been treated so many different ways in school. If I was the type of student that would do such evil thoughts like that, I would have done it, because of the way they treated me. There's a cause and effect to everything. You're doing this, I'm gonna do this. If you don't do this, I wouldn't do this.

Their responses about the two most critical problems were consistent with those of the interview respondents. Safety and violence were identified by 42 percent of interview respondents; and the absence of an adequate learning environment was identified by 15 percent. These responses also relate to the implied lack of viable alternative methods of teaching students with behavioral problems. The youth focus group responses corroborated responses of educators who thought a strong curriculum and smaller learning environments would improve the climate in the school and how those ingredients would begin to resolve the issue of disorder and violence. Finally, the youth focus group participants provided a clearer understanding of implications for not finding effective ways for educating students with behavioral issues.

Beyond the Classroom

When queried about a role for public schools beyond educating the youth, the youth focus group participants did not understand the question and needed an explanation of what was being asked. As an example, the researcher put forth the possibility of administrators making school buildings available 24-hours a day to the community for afterschool programs, sports, and learning centers. The researcher asked the respondents if this was something the schools should sponsor and, if so, would it deter youth violence and would they participate? The following interchange took place:

> Respondent 1: That's a complicated question.
>
> Respondent 2: I think it's true, to a certain extent. Certain people, they're not going to go over there, they're going to do what they want to do.
>
> Researcher: So you don't think the youth would use the building?
>
> Respondent 2: Certain people would, but certain wouldn't. There's always that percent of the youth that's not about that, not going to do that. They might peer pressure some other youth to not go there and do something else.
>
> Researcher: Do you think more students would be involved in school? Do you think there would be less crime, less violence, less kids dropping out of school if the buildings were opened?
>
> Respondent 2: I think it would probably be less. Less crime, less violence, yeah, I don't know how much less, but it would be. It's another option. Instead of doing this, you could go over there. Yeah, there'd probably be less crime, there'd be more kids in school, doing things, activities, and not out on the street fighting or rob somebody. So, yeah.

Respondent 3: Yeah, sure. But like he said, there's always going to be that certain percentage that's going to go against it, that's going to go with it, there's always that apple that gotta be that bad apple.

Researcher: Would you go? Would that interest you?

Respondent 2: Yeah it would, because I play basketball and I play football, when I used to go and play at the Dole Center, 'cause I was playing for the AAU team, we used to travel around, but a certain time, 9 o'clock, 9:30, they close the Dole Center down. And at that time, that's when everybody go in the streets. If it's open to play basketball while security is in it, so it would keep kids off the street, playing what they like, instead of being on the street. That's why I really got arrested, because I used to play sports. After sports, because sports used to really keep me out of trouble, because I used to really put all my mind to it. I play sport after sport, go home, nothing to do, go out on the street, sit with your friends, do what you do. But if that place was still going, you'd still be there. Less crimes, less people in jail, people are happy. That's how I see it.

Researcher: What about you?

Respondent 1: I think it would help, because once you have something to occupy your time then you don't think about doing something violent or planning to rob anywhere, or just occupy your time so you have some sports to play or some activity to participate in.

Students were asked if they preferred to go to the high school in Bronxville. The researcher pointed out that Bronxville High School had all the elements the students described in their ideal school and that the community probably had more available buildings for afterschool activities. One youth said he would not want to go to a school that he never heard about. This answer was a surprise to the researcher, because the school was less than two miles away from the middle school in town. One youngster asked, "Like what? Bronxville over there like by Cross County?" Another student interrupted with, "It's in a wealthy White community." Another youth responded incredulously, "There's going to be segregation!" After assuring the group that the question was only hypothetical, the following interchange took place:

Respondent 1: No, I want them to make one here or in Yonkers so we could walk there. I don't want to go to a wealthy white community where they're gonna have a good school. Like White Plains has one of the best.

Respondent 2: Come on, everywhere where there's 90 percent of Whites and 10 percent of minorities, that's where the best schools is, why's that?

Researcher: So you wouldn't want to go to school there, you just want that kind of school to be in your own neighborhood?

Respondent 2: Yeah, exactly. But it can't happen.

Respondent 2: They're not doing it. Go to [school name], it's 92 percent Black, 5 percent Hispanics, the rest—others—1 percent white. I really looked at the ratio.

Respondent 2: I told you, I love Mount Vernon High School, it's just—it's cool, and White Plains is 96 percent White, 5 percent Black, 1 percent Hispanic. Why is that? Because it's in a White area, where White people pay as much money as they want and the government see that money keep flowing, nobody gotta check up on them, like, "Hey you gotta pay," nah, they keep paying.

Respondent 1: Some of them don't even have it and they want to keep that reputation of White people being wealthy like more White people, so they want to keep it. You know what I mean?

Respondent 2: Rotating, keep a cycle, they want them to be at the top, they don't want them to end up being the minority, and that's why. There's a lot of people that don't have—just like middle class like us, but they go to that school, they give them the resources so that they can be what they want them to be, but they don't give us none. I don't know.

This train of thought went on for several minutes and revealed a sense of apathy and powerlessness among the youth that was consistent with the sense of apathy expressed by adult respondents who participated in the in-depth interview discussions. These young men blamed every negative condition or experience in their lives on Caucasians. When asked to respond to the reality that in spite of the fact that Mount Vernon had a Black mayor, a Black City Council, and a Black Board of Education, the city had one of the lowest performing high schools in the county, one youngster gave the following response:

> Yes, it's a Black town, but keep it in mind; it's a Black town that's being run by somebody that's White. I'm not talking about the mayor, the mayor is Black, but it's being run by a White thought. You know. Either way, it's being run by a White thought, you can't take that out of my mind.
>
> Researcher: Okay, so what if Obama becomes president?
>
> They're going to assassinate him. They're going to assassinate him, I swear to God, they will assassinate him, or they will probably give him some medicine in the food that he eats, he's dead by eating some food poison. Come on, White people, they're really trying to stop us from moving forward.

The responses these young men provided substantiated several findings from the in-depth interviews. First, these young men concurred with 88 percent of respondents who believed that schools could play a role beyond education. They also agreed with several respondents who believed that extracurricular activities would deter crime and violence among young people. Second, general apathy and lack of respect for cultural diversity were the two leading barriers cited by respondents as impediments to building public support for public education. Their interchange provided a vivid illustration of the magnitude of intolerance and apathy that potentially exists among Mount Vernon youth. If the rage heard from these young men accurately represents the sentiments of the broader population, then much work would truly have to be done to bring about a coalition of people in support of public education.

Getting Along

One young man spoke on this subject. He did not believe the public had a good relationship with the public school district. Similar to perceptions expressed by interview respondents, this young man believed the system was closed and only certain people had access. He pointed out that there were a few people who got involved, but that nothing much has been accomplished. He described the relationship in the following way:

> Nah—public school district do their, do their own public school district, do their own. They on their own. And the citizens, they're on their own. They really don't interfere. Only certain people interfere together, interfere and interact with each other, try to make the public school system better. But, it really doesn't, you really don't see that frequently happen. You know. You really haven't had a parent that really concerned about the kid and really asks. . . . You know, but most of the parents, like we said before, don't really, tryin' to themselves in the school system.

When asked if his mother was involved, he said, "I don't think [she] is, because she's not the one attendin'. I am. So it doesn't really matter, as long as I'm gettin' an education."

In addition to corroborating the perception that the public doesn't have a good relationship with its public schools, this young man's comments about his mother are consistent with those respondents who suggested that many students are forced to be their own advocates. Interview respondents described how parents are not involved because they are busy working to make ends meet. These young adult students are expected to have a level of maturity to manage their own educational affairs. Finally, they helped to identify potential new areas for research; for example, under what conditions younger members of the public could be nurtured to become a prepared public willing and available to support its public schools.

Chapter 16

The Teacher Focus Group

Because of the close relationship teachers have with parents and children, there was an interest in understanding teachers' perceptions of the environment in which they were working and the implications for helping children learn. There was also interest in teachers' perceptions of the extent to which the school culture nurtured parent involvement. Our meeting was held at a local church during August 2007 and six classroom teachers participated. Five of the participants currently taught at the same elementary school. Another had also taught at the school but, at the time of the focus group, was teaching at another elementary school within the district.

Four open-ended questions were used to explore some of the findings from the interviews:

1. Why did educators believe the public placed a lower value on public education, lower than respondents who participated in the interviews?
2. What were some key elements of their ideal school?
3. With the absence of leadership cited as the second most critical problem facing the district, to what extent did it affect the learning environment within the school building?
4. Why did education specialists not believe the public owned public schools, given the apparent strong public interest?

The Importance of Education

Based on the interview data, 40 percent of education specialists believed the public ranked the institution of public education as somewhat important or not very important. This was a lower ranking than that given by the other stakeholder groups. In addition, 36 percent of education specialists cited safety as more important to the public than public education. Low taxes and family survival were each identified by 27 percent of education specialists as more important. Although the teacher focus group shared some of the views of interview respondents, the teacher focus group respondents pointed to other causes for their lower-ranking scores.

One respondent took a self-reflective perspective, and questioned if the school district was doing enough to solicit the support of parents:

> I think people care, but I, I really think as a school system we've failed to still reach out to support, and that was again a bigger, important part of public education. I find the reluctance of the school system to provide the opportunities to be supportive before, and I say again, because of my age. My parents were not as educated, but they believed that the school system was going to educate me. So their support was there, right or wrong. I don't find that we—and I'm saying 'we' as part of the public school system—are able to extend the same support. So, therefore, there might be also a reason on our part on why the parents do not feel that they can reach into us to give the support also.

The teacher focus group respondents also described how the low ranking was due to a sense of apathy and disillusionment felt by the public. They described how parents were highly engaged during the struggle against the ICA. During that battle, people knew who they were fighting against. When the Black community won their battle for greater representation, they expected broad and swift changes to take place. Given that changes have not been as transformative as many residents had envisioned, parents and the at-large community struggle with identifying where to take their fight.

One teacher led the following group discussion on how VOTE, a grass roots organization, had had an impact on school and community relations:

> Respondent 1: Get back to that change that I was alluding to, the change of ethnicity, the change of who is considered in power also . . . in

> Mount Vernon, before you had the ICA, which was a powerful organization within Mount Vernon. On the other side, you had—and I want to say based out of Grace Church—you had—oh, what was it called? VOTE? But, no, VOTE didn't really come out of there. But, VOTE was a grassroots organization that started in Mount Vernon, Voices of the Electorate. And people assume that certain things were happening because of the composition of the board and certain schools were neglected and certain schools had certain privileges, opposed to when that board changed. Now the question is one that the community brought up, the color of the board has changed, but the policies haven't changed.
>
> Respondent 2: That's right.
>
> Respondent 4: So, now you don't have as, as the color changed to our color now, we don't even have the same arrows to shoot and say 'Well, what's happening?'

This interchange provides new insights for the causes of apathy within the Black community. It suggests that the Black community has only had experience with fighting injustice or unfairness within a racial context. Blacks were fighting for racial equality against Whites who controlled all the resources. Now that the battle had been won, and the community put people in place to represent their cause fairly, respondents suggested that parents and the at-large community had no idea of how and with whom to fight for improved conditions.

When asked why people fail to take advantage of their privilege to vote to remove ineffective leaders, the group described how the small-town nature of Mount Vernon reduced voting to a popularity contest. The following interchange sums up the teacher focus group respondents' perceptions of this small-town phenomenon:

> Respondent 1: "That's my people! I'm gonna vote for him." "That's my cousin such-and-such" or "That's my third cousin." That's the reason to vote for a person?
>
> Respondent 3: That's why they don't take the time to educate the constituents. Because it doesn't really matter.
>
> Respondent 2: That's right.
>
> Respondent 1: I'm telling you it's A and B. Choose 1.

Respondent 3: Right.

Respondent 1: And you just choose the one that looks like he's a nicer person or you know.

Respondent 3: "My cousin Pookie said he's a good man! So I'm voting for him!"

In summary, the teacher focus group respondents offered a variety of new views on why educators feel the public might not rank public education higher on a scale of importance or why parents fail to transfer their care for their children into meaningful participation. Respondents described a public that is unaware of how to participate in an environment where they are the majority. First, educators suggested that residents lack experience in demanding accountability from a group with whom they closely identify—their Black leaders. Second, many parents do not possess the sophistication needed to leverage their voting power to their advantage. The absence of information and education perpetuates the tendency for residents to take on a small town mindset by making decisions based on familiarity versus the credentials of a given candidate. The new majority lacks experience in being constructively critical of people they put in office and in holding them accountable while maintaining their friendships or long-held relationships. The teachers' responses suggest that this is particularly true when the leaders in power are of the same ethnic group. The new White *minority,* many of whom are part of the bedroom community, lack the political power or the incentive to resist. Instead, they opt out of local education politics and invest their time and other resources in alternative educational settings for their children.

The Ideal School

While 29 percent of interview respondents cited a culture conducive to learning as a key component of their ideal school, and 18 percent cited a dedicated, high quality teaching staff, the teacher focus group respondents cited leadership and parent involvement as key components. In terms of leadership, the focus group respondents expressed a desire for leaders who were open to seeking the input of teachers. They wanted a leader who was more supportive and open to hearing what teachers really need in order to be effective in the classroom.

The following discussion around this issue provides insight into what the teacher focus group believed was missing within their district:

> Respondent 3: I guess I'm tired of administration making decisions for teachers when they have not been in the classroom or they've been out of the classroom for such a long time that they are out of touch with our current needs.
>
> Respondent 5: They taught for two years. Two years and now you're an administrator.
>
> Respondent 1: We do need informed leaders. We don't have that, I don't think. Either they've been doing it that way for ages and that's the way it should be or they flip-flop and they're not really clear on what will happen. So you're flip-flopping with them because, you know, every year there's something new and exciting. But there's no substance. And so that's hard to keep up with.

The teachers also talked about parent involvement as an important element of their ideal school. They described the value of starting relationships with parents soon after the birth of the child. They dreamed of a district with the capacity to work with new parents in the home, helping them to prepare their toddlers to be ready to read upon entering kindergarten. They believed that establishing strong relations early-on made for sustained relationships over time.

> . . . and it makes a parent feel like, "Wow, the community's really cohesive. The school is with me. They're doing this with me." They don't feel like an outsider even if they had a bad experience in school. It would definitely change that attitude toward school if there's that more of a connection. Mount Vernon's small enough to make this happen.

The teacher focus group did not validate key components of the ideal school expressed by respondents who participated in the in-depth interviews. They did, however, provide insight into the type of leadership that would be helpful to them in the classroom. They also provided an example of how they would build a stronger foundation for sustainable partnerships with parents.

An Absence of Leadership

Among interview respondents, there was a lot of discussion about how the political environment in which the district operates affects the work environment. Interview respondents claimed it caused a *domino effect* throughout the entire system. They suggested that a lack of leadership on the part of the Board of Education resulted in their call for an inspiring work environment. There was an interest in knowing the extent to which teachers experienced any domino effect as a result of a perceived absence of leadership.

The teacher focus group respondents described an unhealthy competitive environment where schools are pitted against one another—all competing for the attention of the central office. They discussed principals competing among themselves for school name recognition and how this created a "me" environment. The following interchange is an example of the environment described by teachers:

> Each school is treated like its own fiefdom. I am hoping and I'm excited about hearing from the new superintendent because of some words that he's said. One, he mentioned *teamwork* among all of the schools. That is something that has not truly been implemented in education in Mount Vernon. And because of that lack of teamwork, your scores are published publicly, so now you set up a competition. And the competition in this case is not a win-win for all of Mount Vernon children. I win, you lose. Ha, ha, ha on you. I can squeeze out more money because everybody's flocking to my school. My parents are gonna vote. Opposed to not succeeding and the difference of [school name] being [school name] and a dumping ground for people and teachers and students. So now you have your principals' meeting and some principals don't come. Some principals won't share information. Some principals demand, "I want this," or the superintendent has to be worried about 150 parents appearing at her office.

They also described how the pressure for principals to deliver schools with passing scores on standardized tests pits principals against one another and has a trickle-down effect on the classroom teacher:

> Respondent 5: Well. I think there's a lot of—there's a lot of competition for attention at the highest level. And if we do something spectacular, you will notice us. So I think a lot of our administrators are puppets who just dance so that they can get someone to notice them.

Respondent 3: And I remember a friend of mine, and I've said this before, who was getting ready to start her program in her building [school name], and she sent me some information because we were friends. And so after she had done that, I said, "Oh, this is wonderful! Let me get in touch with the consultant so he can come here." Her principal got wind and her principal told her, "Don't you share what's going on in our building with that building." And I just—it just really hurt me. Because I'm saying to myself, "You should want children to do well. It's not about you."

Respondent 5: It's not about you and your building. If what you're doing in your building is so top secret, you should want it for every child.

Respondent 3: To benefit from whatever wonderful idea is brought in. If you need to hear your name, then fine! We'll say we got it from you. But, come on!

Researcher: Is that widespread?

Several Respondents: Yes, it is.

The teachers described how demeaning it feels to attend teacher meetings at the central office where principals report their results. The teacher focus group respondents viewed these meetings as a "show and tell" event where higher performing schools are celebrated at the expense of lower performing schools. Participants in this focus group describe how some teachers feel patronized:

> If you really want to see the results of that—exactly what we're talking about—come out in September, the first day of school. Come to the meeting that all of the teachers have to go to in Mount Vernon. And look at the show start, the charade, how we call people's names and then the lobbyists for the chair, for which principal is the best one, the stats are up for each school and who's doing well and we're gonna celebrate this principal. And the rest of you, really, you keep on working hard. It is a sad affair. I do not see children coming first.

The teacher focus group participants substantiated responses made by some interview respondents who described an unhealthy competitive environment in which educators were working. Although these educators recognized the value of rewarding principals who produced higher-performing schools, they believed successes were not used as a tool to encourage other schools that did not fare as well. As opposed to perpetuating a collaborative environment that promoted the sharing of best practices, administrators promoted a "me" environment within which principals must compete for attention. The focus group respondents provided an example of how the lack of leadership can trickle-down throughout the system, ultimately to the classroom teacher.

Teachers' Perceptions of Ownership

Among education specialists who participated in the in-depth interviews, only 9 percent believed the public owns public schools. This was significantly lower than responses from other stakeholder groups. There was an interest in understanding the notion of public ownership of public schools from the teachers' perspective. The teacher focus group participants found it difficult to assign the same acknowledgement of ownership across stakeholder groups. As parents, they embraced ownership as their right and as a function of democracy. However, as teachers, it was more difficult to acknowledge the public as owners. The following statement sums up this sentiment of an African American teacher and parent:

> I'm trying to figure out how not to be the teacher, to be the parent and also how to be the resident of Mount Vernon. And I think as a resident of Mount Vernon, I believe that I own the school. As a parent in Mount Vernon, I believe that the school is answerable to me. I'm my child's advocate and you need to respond to me according to—As a teacher, do I think the parents own the school? No.

Teachers did not recognize parents as owners. Parent ownership is, at best, limited to parents who are not confrontational, who are willing to work within the system, and who are willing to serve as advocates for their own children.

The teacher goes on to describe the conditional nature under which she would accept parental ownership:

> So it depends on what I have on at the moment. I will be there to help you, depending on how you approach me. It depends on the approach. If you come in and you own the school and you're gonna tell me what to do because 'I pay you,' well, nothing's gonna get done. You're not going to do that. But on the other hand, if—if you come and you want

> to be able to be a part of the system and you want to help your child, then—then I'm open to that. So it really depends on your approach.

This response validates data received from the in-depth interviews where 31 percent of respondents believed either the public did not own public education or that ownership was conditional. If parents behaved in a certain way, then they had the right to claim ownership. If they did not, they forfeited ownership.

Teachers spoke about leaders who do not promote parental or community ownership. They only build partnerships with those parents who go along with the principal's agenda. They work with parents who do not threaten to challenge the status quo. One respondent described how a young parent stepped forward to head their school's PTA, but, because of conflict with the principal, felt pressured to resign her position.

A respondent provided the following insight on how school culture reinforces the notion that public ownership is conditional:

> We had the great opportunity and I just put it out there. That we had a young person to come into PTA and share a lot of great ideas. She really wanted to do things. She was very excited about things. Unfortunately, when she found out about the way the system works for PTA in the building, she was not pleased. And as much as she tried for change, she ran into a lot of resistance from the head of the building. And that person, you know, the head of the building, made it so uncomfortable to the point that she decided that she didn't want to deal with it anymore and said, "I quit." She was now blackballed from the building.

The teacher focus group participants described how, although there are buildings where principals work in a collaborative way with their PTAs, there are buildings such as their own where PTAs are not strong. Just as principals are rewarded for their performance, parents who conform to a principal's expectations are likewise rewarded. Those who do not are shunned and made to feel uncomfortable. They find that the school culture that does not promote a sense of ownership among parents. Parents are, at best, consumers of education and advocates for their own children. Parental ownership of public schools is conditional; it does not extend to having rights to hold education professionals accountable.

This focus group discussion with teachers from Mount Vernon schools validated much of what was expressed by respondents who participated in the in-depth interviews. It also provided greater insight into why educators feel the public ranks education lower than other priorities. Respondents provided new perspectives on the sense of apathy and disillusionment that exists among residents, how ineffective leadership perpetuates an unhealthy environment that trickles down both to classroom teachers and to parents, and how school culture contributes to educators' perceptions that parental ownership is conditional.

Part Five

From Disenfranchisement to Ownership

Chapter 17

Findings from the Mount Vernon School District

Findings from this study provide a snapshot of public perception of the political landscape in which the MVSD was operating in 2007. Responses from approximately 100 people who participated through interviews and focus groups generated ten findings in four categories: the capacity of the public to take on ownership of public schools; public perceptions of what was taking place in public schools in the district; the public's awareness of its role as owners of public schools; and barriers that would have to be overcome for the public to build sustaining coalitions in support of public schools. The findings that were generated reveal the public's potential for service as a valuable resource for the local public school district.

The Public's Confidence in Public Education

Finding 1: The vast majority of the people of Mount Vernon had a high regard for the institution of public education.

More than 70 percent of the people interviewed were products of public education. Whether they attended segregated public schools in the South or de facto segregated public schools in the North, many respondents recounted fond memories of their public school experience and the important role it played in shaping their lives. Almost all respondents described the high educational standards to which they were held as children. Although many respondents grew up under poor and often inequitable conditions, most described how public education was the cornerstone of their community. More than 64 percent of the people interviewed believed the people in the MVSD would rank public education as a *very important* or an *important* institution.

Finding 2: Residents had a clear sense of the type of educational system they envisioned for their children.

The participants identified several key elements important for their ideal school. More than 29 percent cited a school culture conducive to learning as a critical component, and more than 16 percent cited a dedicated and highly-qualified staff. In addition, 14 percent cited a safe environment and social order, as well as a state-of-the-art physical facility, as important elements of their ideal school. Respondents cited the need for financial and in-kind support from businesses for internships and after-school programs. They also described the role they believed the religious community could play in building an ideal school. The diversity of the community and its small-town characteristics were recognized as major assets for their ideal school.

Perceptions of the State of Public Education in the MVSD

Finding 3: The public was not satisfied with the MVSD's progress towards preparing the city's youth for their future.

In spite of the value the public placed on public education, the sense of confidence and regard for public schools did not extend to the entire MVSD. Many respondents cited the great improvements taking place at the elementary school level. They boasted about increases in student performance on state standardized tests, the district's inventory of Blue Ribbon schools, and its growing national reputation for the excellence of its elementary schools. Despite these tangible improvements, only 17 percent of the people interviewed believed that children who attended schools in the MVSD were being adequately prepared for their future. More than 47 percent of respondents said they were, in fact, dissatisfied in that regard.

Another 28 percent gave the district a mixed review. Both groups had some concerns with high school and middle school grades. Low student test scores, low graduation rates, and an overall lack of order and safety were among specific problems reported by respondents. People who offered a mixed review believed the problems were limited to the middle schools and high schools. In their opinion, only elementary schools were faring well. Some respondents expressed dissatisfaction and disappointment with both secondary and elementary schools. They felt the demands imposed by NCLB encouraged educators to place too much emphasis on passing standardized tests. As a result, the curriculum was designed to build test-taking abilities, rather than to equip students with strong foundational skills. Many believed that this ultimately resulted in children being promoted to the middle school unequipped with the critical thinking skills needed for success at that level.

Finding 4: Residents agreed in identifying the two most critical problems facing the district.

More than 40 percent of the participants identified lack of safety and social order as the most critical problem facing Mount Vernon's public schools, especially at the high schools and middle schools. For example, many believed the MVSD was in denial about crime being a school problem. Administrators failed to understand that the problem with crime and youth violence was a responsibility shared by the community and the school district. The respondents felt that the MVSD was unwilling to accept its share of responsibility. Although some respondents felt the issue of crime in the schools was blown out of proportion, many respondents believed the district was deliberately minimizing incidents taking place on school grounds so as to avoid negative coverage in the press. It was suggested that this happened to the extent of sometimes impeding police investigations.

Respondents also felt there was unwillingness on the part of the district to enforce a no-tolerance policy. They described instances where administrators would overrule decisions made at the building level that were intended to uphold behavior standards. Administrators sometimes felt forced to "give in" to disgruntled parents or special-interest groups by readmitting disorderly students to the classroom. Respondents believed this "backing down" had created a perception of tolerance for violence and disorder, sending the wrong message to the entire education family—parents, staff, and students.

Many believed there was no plan for properly managing situations involving students with behavioral problems and other special needs. There were two points of view on this issue. One was the perception that students who misbehave should be removed from the classroom. Some respondents believed that by their disruptions, these youngsters were risking the education of the entire student body. Others felt that many students who misbehaved were crying out for attention. They suggested that keeping them in school was the only way to keep them from losing their way, and that removing them could do irreversible harm to their lives. Although respondents found credibility in both arguments, many believed that not having a workable plan for educating troubled youth had produced continual social disorder and displayed a pattern of tolerance for misbehavior. As a result, parents were taking their youngsters out of the district after sixth grade at an alarming rate.

Finally, many respondents believed the public was in denial as to the extent that safety and disorder are *community* problems. There were those who believed the behavior of youth to be a result of parents who no longer provided a moral compass for their children. Some felt it was a result of many parents having children at a very early age, when they lacked basic skills in parenting; they described this pattern as "babies raising babies." Others pointed out the absence of important role models in the home, as when fathers are not there for their children. Some felt even certain churches were in denial, as some ministers who were interviewed made the distinction between youth in their congregation and "those" youth causing crime in the community. All in all, respondents believed the community should have accepted greater responsibility for crime involving youth and been more actively involved in finding solutions.

The other critical problem, identified by nearly 24 percent of the people interviewed, was the absence of leadership within the school district as well as within the at-large community. In regard to the school district, respondents believed its school board lacked the vision and the capacity to lead the district into the twenty-first century. Rather than serving as a visionary body, respondents suggested, a board with little or no expertise in educational administration was doing a great deal of micromanaging. As a result, superintendents had been marginalized, making them ineffective in running day-to-day operations, while the board continued to neglect its policy-setting role. Respondents described an environment where administrators at the highest levels within the district were forced to placate the board in order to get things done. They described how these actions resulted in a domino effect impacting all levels of management as well as the teaching staff. Ultimately, lack of leadership was permitting an environment of retribution that distracted employees, both teachers and administrators, from their main responsibility—educating children. Instead, staff and faculty were devoting their attention to constantly searching for political cover, managing dynamics with superiors and, increasingly, making politically expedient decisions and judgments.

Respondents described a board that operated as if public schools were for their own special interest group—the Black community. It was displaying blatant intolerance of people not of the same group. Rather than demanding a higher degree of excellence and accountability from all employees, that body was perceived as furthering the environment of divisiveness within the school system. For example, respondents described a school culture in which problems with the teaching staff were blamed on those White educators who were said to be insensitive to the needs of Black and Latino children. Respondents recognized that there were some professionals on staff who were burned out, insensitive, or uninterested in teaching children of color. However, they believed the board should have demanded that administrators weed out ineffective staff, regardless of who they were. But this was nearly impossible, given a working environment fraught with favoritism and blatant cronyism. As opposed to uniting a public around the district, respondents described how actions of some board members perpetuated the polarization of the community, a phenomenon that had already existed for many years.

Respondents described Black churches as having undue influence in shaping education policies and practices. They had become, in the eyes of many, the new Black political machine, with ministers using their power to control who sat on the board and to secure important positions for their parishioners. As opposed to the board inspiring a collective public to embrace the district, the board continued to operate as if it represented one constituency group—the Black community and, especially, the Black churches. Many suggested that this helped continue the community's historic polarization. Absence of leadership was cited by many respondents as creating a crisis in the district—a situation demanding immediate attention.

Finally, respondents discussed the absence of public support for public schools. First, they described the absence of much-needed support from middle class residents who lived in the Mount Vernon area as a bedroom community—using city resources, but taking no responsibility for local public schools. Respondents also described families who struggled every day with family survival issues and simply did not have the ability to focus their attention on public education. Several respondents sympathized with working and poor parents who have other legitimate priorities. However, they were aware of the consequences of the absence of this important segment of the public, as these families often have children with the greatest needs, requiring the investment of many resources. Respondents felt that non-participation of both working-class and of poor families had had a detrimental effect on the quality of education within the MVSD.

Finding 5: The public lacked confidence in the existing decision-making process.

When asked about how things got done for education in Mount Vernon, 79 percent of respondents replied that things got done either behind closed doors or through a formal process that served basically as a facade for decisions already made behind closed doors. Almost 60 percent of people who answered this question felt that, whatever the process of getting things done was, it did not bode well for public trust or represent good business practice. Respondents also described a process unfriendly to the public. Among the examples given by respondents were late meetings, long drawn-out executive sessions, and items important to parents scheduled at the end of long agendas.

Finding 6: The public did not have a good relationship with its public school district.

More than 80 percent of the people interviewed believed the public had either a poor relationship with the MVSD or no connection at all. However, progress had been made toward improving one-on-one relationships. Although respondents felt the relationship between the public and the school district was poor, 54 percent noted that their own, or their organization's, relationship with the MVSD was either good or improving. Comments were also made regarding the positive changes taking place at the Board of Education center. Some reported refreshing signs of a newfound respect for the public.

The Public's Role as Owners of Public Schools

Finding 7: The public was largely unaware that public schools belonged to them and that their ownership was a function of their living in an American democracy.

Only 18 percent of the public believed it owned its public schools and understood that their ownership was a function of living in a democracy. These respondents were clear that no one could take ownership from them, and that it was not something they could forfeit. Most respondents accepted the fact that the public might own public schools. However, almost 61 percent of respondents believed that public ownership of public schools had been usurped by another entity. Even after several reiterations of the concept of public ownership, 14 percent of all respondents—across all stakeholder groups—were adamant that public schools did not belong to the public.

Finding 8: Respondents supported the idea of building a coalition in support of public education.

The description of the coalition put forth by the researcher represented a cross-section of people from government, the school district, community-based organizations, businesses, and the at-large community. In spite of a negative depiction of the public's relationship with the school district, 92 percent of respondents were optimistic about the possibility of building a coalition in support of public education. Education specialists were among the least enthusiastic. Many educators believed that only under certain conditions could a coalition be successful. Nonetheless, respondents across all stakeholder groups—including educators—were in support of working collectively to build public support for higher-performing schools.

Finding 9: Respondents had a good sense of what they wanted in a citywide organization.

Respondents concurred on the key issues around which this coalition should rally. Among the respondents who answered the question, 44 percent believed the group should rally around the demand for excellence in public education, while 20 percent suggested the groups should rally around promoting parent and community involvement. Another 48 percent of residents strongly believed that the leadership for this organization should originate among parents and/or the community at large. Respondents also wanted an inclusive organization that would encompass representatives from the new and emerging underrepresented populations, as well as youth and the elderly. Finally, it was very important for the coalition to be financially independent with a capacity for being sustained for a long time.

Barriers to Sustaining an Educational Coalition

Finding 10: Respondents achieved consensus on the barriers that had to be overcome in order to build a strong coalition.

In spite of the enthusiasm expressed, respondents were very clear about the tremendous amount of work involved in building a citywide coalition. They described several barriers to be overcome in order to successfully build a coalition. Bias, discrimination, and the lack of tolerance of differences were described by almost 38 percent of respondents as major impediments to building an effective organization. It is ironic that respondents named the city's greatest strength—its diversity—as a factor most detrimental to their efforts. The other barriers identified by 27 percent of respondents were people with personal agendas, inflated egos, and an overall lack of cooperative spirit. Complicating the picture still further, respondents described another of the city's great strengths, its close-knit, small-town character, as another obstacle to building an effective city-wide coalition for public education.

Chapter 18

Causes for Disenfranchisement

Misguided Attempts to Manage a Broken System versus Overseeing Systemic Reform

Like many Black-led communities in America that continue to struggle under conditions of poverty and distressed public school systems,[1] Mount Vernon provides harsh lessons for understanding why meaningful educational reforms and transformation of public schools have been slow to materialize. The strong coalitions that had once been established to create high quality and equitable public schools have dwindled over time, leaving behind a disappointed public. This once-eager public had expected their newly elected Black leadership to represent the interests of a historically disenfranchised people. They had expected their leadership to be accountable and to have the capacity to transform public schools at a rapid pace. They also anticipated policy changes that would result in a more equitable distribution of resources to schools throughout the district—changes that would replace hiring practices based on nepotism and patronage with professional qualifications and objective standards. Members of this public also anticipated a multicultural curriculum that reflected the heritage of people within the community to be implemented district-wide. Yet, after more than a decade of new leadership, many were displeased and frustrated by the pace of educational reform, leading one to ask why that reform had been slow to take hold in Mount Vernon.

One source of delay is found in the situation at the time the Black community won control of the Board of Education. The new leadership inherited a broken system, one that safeguarded the status quo. That status quo was not designed to offer an equitable education to all Mount Vernon children. Like many schools in the north, Mount Vernon public schools had operated within the context of de facto segregation through the 1960s. Schools on the north side of Mount Vernon accommodated the needs of White children who lived in segregated, White, middle class neighborhoods, while schools on the south side were reserved for the Black community. Nor was the status quo designed to operate efficiently based on fair and objective practices or sound pedagogy. The new leadership did little to replace the organizational systems that protected the previous delicate balance of power.

In spite of the need for a major overhaul of the teaching staff, the board did little to address policies for tenure. Their failure to effectively negotiate with the teachers' union to reform tenure policies prevented weeding out ineffective educators or rewarding effective ones. After more than a decade, 66 percent of lead classroom teachers were White educators with records of long tenure. The board's lack of progress in correcting the racial imbalance among teachers was viewed as upholding policies that protected ineffective teachers. In addition, hiring practices were perceived to rely more on whom applicants knew and to what sorority or church they belonged than on their qualifications. As far as the public was concerned, nepotism and association continued to trump hiring practices based on competence and what was right for children. In essence, the board was perceived as doing too little to change policies and simply practicing the same unfair policies that existed under the previous political machine.

The demand for a multicultural curriculum had been the mantra for school reform during the community's struggle for greater representation on the school board, and the Parker School served as a model. Located on the south side, the Parker School had initiated a multicultural curriculum model based on higher academic standards. Student performance at the Parker School showed high achievement levels, but many people felt petty board politics and personality conflicts made it difficult to sustain the program. The school board was also blamed for the failure to expand the curriculum to other schools within the district.

In spite of the board's efforts to create an equitable school system by pouring capital improvement dollars into south side schools, in the absence of policies that ensured more equitable distribution of resources, the public perceived the allocation of resources within the district to be inequitable, favoring schools on the north side. Although the Parker School was recognized as one of the best schools in the district, many people felt that the resources and recognition Parker received were still less than what the north side schools received.

From the public's perspective, it also appeared that things got done behind closed doors with the Board of Education over-utilizing its privilege to conduct business in executive sessions. Even if the board were making headway in breaking down systems that impeded reform, the absence of transparency at the policy-making level made the actions of those in power appear suspicious and underhanded. Absent transparency, public opinion leaned toward overall dissatisfaction, both with their political leaders and the state of their public schools.

Although the fight for control of public schools had been waged by the Black community, a cross-section of groups constituted the important coalitions needed to usher in the new regime in the city government as well as on the school board. Latinos are the second largest and fastest-growing population in Mount Vernon, with Latino children representing 12 percent of enrollment in the MVSD. Yet little had been done to include this group in education debates, a failure that further divided the community along racial lines. As opposed to uniting the public support of systemic change for the benefit of all Mount Vernon's children, the board's neglect had resulted in greater fragmentation, which greatly impeded progress toward school reform.

A new Black political machine—heavily influenced by Black clergy—was perceived as maintaining the status quo. The effort on the part of the new regime to manage a broken system and play by the same rules was seen as just as detrimental as the former political machine led by the ICA. Thus, the new regime lost credibility in the eyes of the public, who felt a sense of betrayal by the people whom they had trusted to safeguard the public's interest. The public, in turn, found little incentive to sustain important coalitions and remain engaged in the process of education politics. Overall, there was a missed opportunity to use the public mandate for equitable public schools to rebuild public schools within the MVSD by bringing the community together around public education.

A Public Ill-equipped to Sustain its Role

Another reason that reform has been slow lay in the public's history of conflict with the MVSD since the days of the ICA regime. Although the

Black community fought against the inequities that were perpetrated by the ICA—inequities that were perceived as a threat to the lifeblood of the community—their work did not end when it gained control over the MVSD in 1999.[2] This was when their work was supposed to begin—an optimal time for an entire community to rebuild its public schools. But Mount Vernon's Black community had had little experience in participating in governance, as they were historically on the periphery and fighting for the right of access. This relative inexperience combined with their leaders' failure to recognize the challenges their new positions posed and to redefine their roles accordingly, severely delayed the process of education reform.

The public had been ill-equipped in making a transition from a position of disenfranchisement to the role of ownership, because they lacked *awareness of their role as owners of public schools.* Only 19 percent of the people we interviewed understood that the public owned public schools and that this right was a function of their living in a democracy. A closer look at our cross-analysis of stakeholder groups revealed that only seven percent of elected and appointed officials and other groups that influence education policy in Mount Vernon understood the public to be the legitimate owners of public schools. Consequently, leaders whose function is to serve the public lacked a sense of accountability to the public they served. This disconnection between the public and its representatives made it difficult to push for school reform. Among administrators and educators paid by the public to oversee their interests, only three percent understood that the public owned public schools. Rather than of the public at large, these educators see public schools mainly as the concern of parents—in particular, parents whose children attend public schools within the district. The district's effort to build important school and community relations had been focused on the involvement of parents at the individual level, i.e., in their own children's educational journey. Although this was a very important component of community-school relations, education specialists failed to see the bigger picture that makes them accountable to the public at large.

The exclusion of the vast majority of citizens who comprised the public slowed the process of education reform, because the public took little interest in investing in a system of which they were not a part. Only three percent of the at-large community—that is, people with no official connection to public schools and who represent the vast majority of the Mount Vernon public—expressed awareness of the public's role as owners of public schools. This group, in particular, displayed a profound unawareness of the power the public possessed. They didn't believe they owned public schools and they didn't have a clue as to how to go about holding accountable the people they elected or hired to serve them.

In addition, the public found it difficult to move from a position of disenfranchisement to a role of ownership, because of their inability to hold their Black leaders accountable. Some members of the Black community expressed disappointment with the performance of some members of the Board of Education and other elected and appointed officials. They found themselves in a quandary when being critical of their own Black leaders. The fight for equality in America has been a unifying force for African Americans and other disenfranchised people of color. This community built strong coalitions over the years that were necessary for survival and for advancement. In spite of the fact that the issues of racial equality and access have been won in Mount Vernon, and much potential access to resources is controlled by people of color, African Americans have not achieved a significant shift in their social and economic conditions. Similarly, little improvement has been made in education, at least in terms of the district's graduation rates. African Americans now find themselves opposing the very people who fought alongside them in their struggle for equality.

Many members of the Black community have not reached a sufficient comfort level to demand accountability from their elected officials. There is an unresolved conflict between their sense of loyalty to "their people" and their need to demand accountability from them. Rather than speaking out against elected officials whom they perceive as supporting policies and practices that do not represent the public's interest, the public abstains from the education debate. Voter turnout for Board of Education matters is a further indication of the feelings of frustration, powerlessness, and disillusionment with the process. Voter turnout is low—six to eight percent—so low that fewer than 3,000 votes were needed to kill a referendum on an annual school budget that proposed modest increases in spending.

Although public participation is low, there is some participation. For example, although Parent Teacher Associations (PTAs) operate at varying degrees of effectiveness, there is an active PTA and PTA Council. There are also independent groups, such as the Mount Vernon Concerned Parents and Community Forum, the Mount Vernon Education Foundation, Community that Cares, Family Ties, and Fleetwood Neighborhood Association. In spite of the presence of these and other groups, there is a lack of public trust in many organizations claiming to represent the public.

Some members of the public who attend board meetings are actively involved in the local education debate. Yet many people question their motives and are turned off by some of the tactics they use to express their dissatisfaction with school policies. They find this more vocal public disconcerting and are not inspired by them. So instead of moving toward greater participation in collective action, they choose to revert to a state of virtual disenfranchisement—electing to abstain from voting on educational issues, attending public board meetings, or participating in any effort to forge a citywide coalition in support of education reform.

Familiarity versus Changing Needs

The public has also been slow to respond to the changing needs of the district. Progress is slowed by the inability of the community to identify and elect representatives with the special abilities needed to manage a school district. The political agenda for the twentieth century demanded advocacy skills—the capacity to articulate the community's need for equal representation on the school board. When candidates with this ability were identified and elected to serve in that function, they were viewed as having done a fine job representing the public's interest. Yet several people described the newly-elected Board of Education as unaware of broader issues or the sweeping powers it possessed. Members were viewed as caught up in petty politics or activities that enhanced their personal political careers. Respondents also spoke about the board members' disinterest in conferring with experts in the field who might help in making decisions on such issues as major multimillion-dollar construction projects, educational curricula, and complex areas of law and contract compliance.

Like major business organizations, Mount Vernon needs to respond to the changing demands of the new century. The public should now require new skills of the people it elects and appoints to serve as guardians of one of the city's most valuable assets. In addition to being the primary vehicle for preparing Mount Vernon youth for their future, the MVSD is a $98 million enterprise that serves as the city's major economic engine. In order to affect change in public schools, the public needs representatives in policymaking positions with expertise in the areas of public education policy, law, economics, finance, and labor relations. This is not to suggest advocacy is no longer important, but that the public needs to do a better job of recognizing those skills that are needed to transform their schools, and to develop important political coalitions to ensure that their needs are met. If their elected leaders fail to engage the expert help needed to deal with such complex issues, the public must demand that they do so.

This study suggests that the public is not scrutinizing its candidates for these abilities. As opposed to critically examining what is needed and then judging potential candidates on their ability to meet new demands, voters are making decisions based on personal acquaintance. For example, more than 75 percent of the people we interviewed had lived in Mount Vernon for over 27 years. Families that have lived in the city for four and five generations have built strong relationships over the years. Decisions about whom to elect are more often based on candidates' affiliations than on their skill set. In addition, some members of the Board of Education have held their positions for more than 20 years. The issue of term limits is not even addressed out of deference to individuals whose relationships with board members have been established over time.

The reluctance of the public to shift their voting patterns and elect people to office based on objective criteria has hindered their ability to bring about education reform. More has to be done to depersonalize the process of selecting new leadership and to move away from decision making based on familiarity—whether from family connections, political loyalty, or religious affiliation. All of these factors have taken precedence over the needs of children and their right to a quality education. As a result, education reform has been delayed.

The Decline of Middle Class Involvement

Another factor that has delayed the process of education reform has been the decline of the middle class involvement in public schools. In communities where the public plays a key role in support of its public schools, middle class homeowners recognize the connection between maintaining high-performing schools and their property taxes and values. Whether or not their children attend public schools, they recognize the importance of investing in excellent schools, so they build ongoing coalitions to support them. In the case of Mount Vernon, the link between property values and public schools has not been strong enough to keep the middle class involved.

The loss of this important constituency with its political clout has been a huge blow to the formation of a new public in Mount Vernon and any attempt to usher in reform. As in many urban communities, the racial shift in the political power structure resulted in the mass exodus of the White middle class. Although a large segment of the middle class chose to remain in Mount Vernon, many of these families, both Black and White, gave up on public schools in the MVSD and selected private schools for their children. Others sent their children to select elementary schools on the north side with the intent to remain in the system only until their children reached the age for middle and high school.

In Mount Vernon, this abandonment by the middle class has led to the phenomenon called *bright flight*—the loss of the highest-achieving Black and White students. From 25 to 30 percent of students who graduate from elementary school do not then enroll in the district's middle school. In addition to suffering this numerical loss, the district's public schools, especially at the middle school and high school levels, are increasingly occupied by students who are economically deprived.

With public schools now led by a Black political machine, the fate of this important institution was viewed by many who participated in this study as a public school district for a poor, disenfranchised, and predominately Black population. There is sharp disagreement over who is at fault—parents, school board members, or school officials. There is a segment of the public whose goal is to keep property taxes low by limiting financial support of public schools. Many do not depend on the public schools to educate their children; others are older adults who no longer have children in the district. In addition, many members of the public simply question the value of public schools in the district and the degree to which investments should be poured into such a *failed* system. This devaluation of public schools in the district has resulted in the fragmentation of the public into groups with opposing objectives. Rather than coalitions that support education reform, the city is seeing coalitions form that oppose investing the resources needed for systemic change.

Working within the State Organizational Structure

The MVSD is also embedded within a network of public school districts that extends throughout the State of New York. The MVSD is bound by state and federal policies, such as the No Child Left Behind (NCLB) guidelines, that define the parameters within which the school district must operate. Yet, Mount Vernon's inability to build important coalitions at the local level makes it difficult to affect change at the state level where resources are available to foster education reform.

The Campaign for Fiscal Equity is an example of what can be done through effective coalition-building. This organization is a New York City advocacy group which challenged the state's fiscal policy. It waged a ferocious legal battle that resulted in the New York Supreme Court ordering the State of New York to develop a new fiscal policy. The Court mandated that this new policy be based on need, so that the State could ensure adequate resources would be available to prepare the poorest children for their future. This change in fiscal policy has far-reaching implications for urban communities like the MVSD based on the *needs* of its student population, and the MVSD stands to gain millions of dollars in subsidies to build the types of ideal schools that so many respondents in this study described. Although some progress has been made in receiving increased state aid, the State continues to govern the allocation of resources by an inequitable fiscal policy. In spite of this potential change in fiscal policy to the benefit of communities like Mount Vernon, the need for fiscal reform was identified by only 10 percent of respondents we interviewed; no one we interviewed talked specifically about the Campaign for Fiscal Equity or its struggle to change state fiscal policy. This included leaders in government, leaders in school administration, leaders in the church, and leaders in the community.

In the absence of a united coalition in support of public schools, the Mount Vernon public has been unable to change its relationship within the larger state organizational structure. As a result, its access to the resources needed to deliver high quality schools is severely compromised, further hindering education reform.

Leadership and Important Infrastructures

Although our findings reveal a public that cares strongly about the institution of public education, we also find a public lacking the essentials needed to govern their public schools—an absence of leadership across all stakeholder groups and an absence of important infrastructures necessary for sustained reform. Although there are leaders within the Mount Vernon community, no single individual was recognized by the public across all stakeholder groups as an advocate for education without political or personal motives. No single group, organization, or governmental entity was identified as an unequivocal advocate for Mount Vernon public schools. In short, there is no one place the public can turn to for credible information on the state of public schools and the policies and practices that shape this important institution.

Reforms in education in the United States have taken place when the public formed coalitions in support of a grassroots agenda for change. These coalitions have had the strong backing of organizations with important infrastructures needed to sustain educational campaigns. The fight for universal education was won as a result of the emergence of a public in central cities. Members of the business community, organizing at the national level, had equipped the public in local communities with educational, legal, and other resources needed to inject their voice into the debate for public schools. Likewise, the fight to end government-supported segregation occurred when the public successfully built a national coalition in support of integrated schools. Various organizations, including the NAACP, the religious community, and many other national and local institutions provided the infrastructure necessary to sustain those political and legal battles. The public depended on these institutions to break down powerful systems designed to maintain the status quo.

By the 1990s, the Mount Vernon public had far less support from these traditional institutions. The NAACP has weakened over the years. Shifts in its ideology, loss of financial support from major contributors, reduction in revenue generated from its national membership drive, and disputes within the organization all contributed to the loss of this very important institution that once served as a major voice for the public in the fight for social justice. The National Urban League, another strong supporter of public education, shifted its work to providing direct service with less emphasis on political advocacy. These changes on a national level have had a major impact on local communities, such as Mount Vernon, and the ability of the public to sustain the momentum for reform at the local level. The Mount Vernon public won its political battle for equity, but the new leadership inherited a broken public school system and took the helm without the infrastructure needed to sustain coalitions that could demand accountability and usher in change.

Finally, although the support the public received from the religious community expanded through the 1990s and the early part of the twenty-first century, that support was not nearly as effective as it was during the Civil Rights Movement. By 1999, the Black clergy was leading that charge almost single-handedly. Thus, at the outset of the twenty-first century, at a time when the MVSD could have benefitted from a multicultural base of support from religious and other advocacy groups, there was little upon which the new majority could depend to sustain itself as a political force for education reform.

Chapter 19

The Role of Black Churches

Religion is an important part of life in the Mount Vernon community; the pulpit is a powerful platform for reaching masses of people. In Mount Vernon, some congregations, such as the Grace Baptist Church and the Greater Centennial AME Zion Church, each have congregations in excess of 5,000 parishioners. The Black Church is the backbone of the Black community of Mount Vernon, and Black clergy enjoy high levels of reverence. Black ministers in Mount Vernon are a driving force in mobilizing the community, and some members of the clergy are even influential in swaying members of their congregations to cast their vote strategically for candidates that the clergy may personally endorse. Yet the political influence of the church has diminished over the years. Blacks have moved into integrated middle class communities in other sections of the county, while maintaining membership to a local church. As the Black Church becomes more regionalized, its influence at the polls diminishes.[1]

Loyalty as an Impediment to Reform

At the turn of the twenty-first century, religious leaders and their lay representatives dominated the Mount Vernon Board of Education, but in 2010, none ran for seats on that board. Many interviewees suggested that candidates' church affiliation often took precedence over their qualifications to represent the best interests of the community. That is, pastors may encourage their parishioners to vote for their own favorite candidate or candidates from a particular congregation. Some ministers are viewed as using their influence to secure jobs for their parishioners or to gain access to school administrators for parishioners who have problems in the district. Respondents recognize how using influence to gain access is an effective tool, but they criticize the use of this strategy to support candidates based on their affiliation instead of their competence or demonstrated ability to deliver results. Some have argued that the fight for equity was won by the entire community—not by a few select churches—and that the "wealth" of those victories should be spread around. These actions have been viewed by many people with whom we spoke as heavy-handed on the part of the ministers and have contributed to the sense of frustration felt by the public. Again, as opposed to speaking out and holding their religious leaders accountable, the public withdraws and, out of deference to spiritual leaders, relinquishes its role as owners of public schools and its obligation to hold its leaders accountable. Thus, the issue of loyalty taking precedence over accountability is a major impediment to education reform.

Fragmentation versus Unity

The Black Church in Mount Vernon has been at the helm of the community's struggle for equality. Since 1925, the Black Church has served as the moral compass for African Americans and Caribbeans who migrated to Mount Vernon. In the 1930s, Black ministers led the fight for better housing and, in the 1960s, they led the fight for civil rights and the fight against de facto segregation. During the 1980s, the clergy was instrumental in supporting the public's demands for equal representation on the Board of Education and in policy-making positions within the district's school administration. In the 1990s, the clergy responded to the call to serve in public office, and the public used its political might to elect them as board trustees. By 2005, the clergy and their lay representatives dominated the seats on the Mount Vernon Board of Education.

The role of the clergy was quite clear from the eighteenth to the twentieth century—to serve as the moral compass for the community and to fight for social justice. The fight for equality was consistent with that role. In the twenty-first century, where re-segregation is occurring at a rapid pace, the clergy found itself in the precarious situation of overseeing a public school system that continued to fall short of public expectations. Now, the increased visibility of the clergy in civic leadership has led to what is perceived as a shift of its moral compass.

Findings from this study suggest that the unblemished reputation of the Black Church comes into question as the public begins to see the

Black Church's role as overseer of public schools as part of the problem rather than the solution. This perspective is clearly not universal, as sectors within the community believe otherwise; that is, they believe members of the clergy have done their best to bring civility and order to the education debate. This has led to fragmentation of public perception of one of Mount Vernon's most important and influential institutions—the Black Church. This comes at a time when the need for solidarity is paramount.

It is now uncertain what the role of the religious community will be in the twenty-first century as re-segregation shifts the balance of power and the issues of equity and access are no longer unifying forces. Some religious leaders have expressed concern about what they consider to be the loss of the clergy's role as the moral compass for the community. Others want the clergy to avoid direct involvement in school as well as city politics, because the nature of secular politics requires difficult decisions that may not be perceived as being in the best interest of the community. They point out that it is difficult for members of the clergy to maintain their moral independence in the eyes of the public when they join coalitions that compromise to achieve desired outcomes.[2] Thus, many people expressed the importance of the church's moving away from secular leadership and resuming its role as moral compass. There was also a broadly based call for healing the community.

Others spoke about the need for Black ministerial leadership to deemphasize its role as *Black clergy* and use its influence to build a base of inter-denominational religious leadership—reaching out to diverse religions in the city—especially in the emerging Latino community. There are the traditional Black Christian-based churches—Baptists, Anglicans, Evangelicals, African Methodists, Episcopalians, United Methodists, Apostolic faiths, and Pentecostals, to name a few. There are also Muslim denominations and Jewish congregations. There are *large* churches with networks and *small*, storefront churches and their networks. These various religious groups have had difficulty working under one umbrella. Not having a united front among Black religious institutions has made it even more difficult to build a sustained inter-denominational effort that would include Latino, Muslim, and Jewish bodies. The religious community was at its highest point during the Civil Rights Era when clergy crossed religious lines to bring about the end to de facto segregation. The absence of that united front has had a toll on the community and its ability to form important coalitions in support of education reform.

Regionalization of Congregations

Another issue with which the Black Church struggles is the regionalization of their congregations and its effects on local school politics. Historically, its churches were local and ministered to local congregations. The end of de facto desegregation in the 1960s offered African Americans greater choices among communities in which to live. As urban centers experienced an outward migration of the White middle class in the mid-twentieth century, they also experienced the out-migration of the Black middle class. Although Black families moved to other communities, many maintained their membership at the churches where they previously resided. As a result, large segments of the Black congregations of churches in Mount Vernon are middle-class Blacks who live in other parts of the region. In addition, as African Americans have experienced economic gains, more families are sending their children to private schools. As a result, it is not uncommon to find congregations in Mount Vernon in which a large majority of the members live in other parts of the Tri-state area and do not send their children to public schools. Either they choose alternative educational settings for their children, or they are older people whose children have already finished their elementary education. Thus, in the course of our interviews, a few pastors we interviewed were quite clear in pointing out that children in public schools, especially those who are troublesome, were not "their" children.

Although this economic prosperity can be viewed as a plus for African Americans, it has resulted in a public with a high regard for the institution of public education in general, but one split on the value of public schools in the district. For example, while 78 percent of all respondents who had children indicated that their children went to public schools, only 42 percent of Mount Vernon respondents with children indicated that their children attended public schools within the MVSD. These findings bring into focus the potential for conflicting priorities among congregations about the importance of public schools within the district. They also create dilemmas for the clergy in terms of what role the clergy should play in education policy while attempting to minister to large and politically diverse congregations.

While the time is ripe for coalition-building in support of public schools, Black churches are ministering to congregations with potentially conflicting priorities that may constitute major voting blocks. These conditions have resulted in an ill-defined role for the Black Church at a time when its control over the outcome of local school politics is diminishing.

Perspectives of the United Black Clergy

Insofar as there was no built-in method for measuring the degree to which public perceptions were accurate representations, we identified people who were at the forefront of education politics within the MVSD and engaged them in a dialogue about the public's perceptions. This led us to the leadership of the United Black Clergy (UBC). While the UBC agreed with much of the analyses concerning the role of the UBC, especially as it pertains to having attempted to fix a failed system, they pointed out that it was never the UBC's intent to create a Black ICA or to be an extension of the ICA. On the contrary, they noted deliberate efforts on the part of the UBC to dismantle any political arm.

One example was the decision to dismantle the Coalition for the Empowerment of People of African Ancestry (CEPAA), which was an expansion of VOTE. While VOTE was a coalition of grassroots residents fighting for greater representation on the district's school board, CEPAA was a cross-section of coalitions that had been forged by the Black Church to build public support for equitable public schools. Once it had become clear that the Black community had won the battle for equal representation, and because the Black community did not want to develop a new political machine, the CEPAA was dismantled.

Another example given by the UBC was the decision to move away from serving as trustees on the Board of Education. By 2008, no members of the clergy served on the Board. It was not that Black clergy could not win those seats or that its capacity to get out the vote was minimized. Rather, according to the UBC, it was a deliberate attempt to move away from taking a leadership role in school politics and in endorsing school board candidates.

The UBC also contended that it had fought for better standards for hiring in the district—standards not based largely on familiarity or church affiliation. They pointed out how the agenda for school board meetings had changed under the new Black leadership. Under the rule of the ICA, agenda items at public meetings focused on contracts between vendors and the district. When the new leadership came on board, the agenda shifted to basic issues that affect classrooms—curriculum, quality of education, teaching staff, and physical plants.

Another area where the UBC felt public perception may not have been accurate is the so-called *exclusivity* of the UBC. They contend that no minister, regardless of the size of his or her congregation, was excluded from being a member. Yet, despite many overtures on the part of the UBC, some ministers chose to decline its call to participate.

We also spoke with a number of former administrators. Although some agreed with the public's perceptions, there were those who felt the board operated with a high level of naïveté. A consistent theme among these former administrators was that the board never really understood its role nor the power it possessed to transform the system. These administrators suggest that there was a sad innocence among some members of the board who may have wanted to do the right thing but simply lacked an understanding of running a complex organization. So they micromanaged and dealt with what they understood—never really seeing the big picture.

Our post-survey discussions with the UBC and former administrators served to reveal the extent of the breakdown in communication between the public and its leaders within the MVSD. They also provided a glimpse of how the public as well as its leaders had difficulty transitioning into the role of owners of public schools.

Chapter 20

A New Beginning for Building Public Support for Public Schools

The findings from this study highlight many areas in which work needs to be done to galvanize the Mount Vernon public into action. Given the fact that absence of leadership was identified as one of the most pressing problems facing the city school district, this chapter discusses the type of leadership that might prove successful in the Mount Vernon School District.

A Role for the Office of the Mayor

The Mount Vernon Board of Education is a separate legal entity headed by a superintendent who reports to the board of trustees—the school district's governing body. From a legal perspective the mayor has no authority over the district; the role of city government is limited to levying taxes to support the district's annual budget. Although the school budget is the municipality's largest expenditure, the mayor has no authority to demand accountability for school district performance. The local school district has its own ordinances for governance, with separate departments for personnel, finance, and other administrative functions. This model for governance emerged in the twentieth century and was designed to protect public schools from 'city hall' politics.[1] Like the majority of the nation's public schools, Mount Vernon operated—and still operates—under this type of governance.

Over the last decade, mayors of large cities have moved beyond the traditional approach to city governance to what is called *integrated gov-*

ernance. In addition to being accountable to the public for efficient operation of police and fire departments, and delivery of sanitation and other public services, mayors in cities like New York, Boston, and Washington, D.C., have actively sought to win governing authority over city schools. These mayors take the position that city government should be held accountable for city schools. Therefore, they are no longer willing to stand on the sidelines, without the power to demand accountability from the public schools—in most instances the largest expenditure in their city budget. They have moved aggressively to make schools accountable to the authority of city government by removing legal arrangements that allow schools to operate as islands unto themselves. These mayors argue that integrated governance facilitates delivery of comprehensive services that advance quality of life for city residents. Because public schools are essential to economic growth and development and the enhancement of quality of life of a city's residents, mayors across the country have looked to the integrated governance model to obtain greater influence in the governance of public schools within their municipalities.[2]

Integrated governance is the twenty-first century model being adopted by many cities with a history of underperforming public schools. Among the first to use this approach were the mayors of Boston in 1992, Chicago in 1995, Cleveland in 1998, and New York in 2002.[3] But integrated governance had not always succeeded. Baltimore schools had operated under this form of governance for years when, in 1997, Maryland state officials, frustrated at Baltimore's ineffective reform efforts, intervened. Maryland's governor and legislature moved away from relying on that city's office of the mayor as the agency primarily responsible for school oversight. It reshaped relationships in a way that reduced the mayor's authority over the schools. Maryland moved in a direction opposite to integrated governance, e.g., back to a more traditional approach.[4] Washington, D.C. had also tried the integrated governance approach. In 2000, voters approved a referendum that radically changed the way school board members were selected, thus giving the mayor a stronger hand in school governance.[5] By 2006 its integrated governance model had ended. In 2004, Detroit voters who had moved to an integrated governance structure in 1999 reverted to the traditional model.[6] However there are several cities where some variation of an integrated governance model has been adopted and continues to operate. Among these are New York; Hartford; New Haven; Trenton; Jackson, Mississippi; Boston and Cleveland.

Clearly our research does not justify our suggesting that integrated governance is a solution for the city of Mount Vernon. What we do suggest is that its leadership at least explores integrated governance as an alternative approach. A modest beginning would be for the mayor to form a task force that would examine the merits of integrated governance and the extent to which it might benefit the Mount Vernon community.

Critics of the situation in Mount Vernon have maintained that since citizens are the voice for public schools, that the public has a right to elect its officials—that the public, not the mayor, should elect school trustees. Our entire study supports this position. Should integrated governance be used as a strategy to reform public schools, it would increase the mayor's authority in the operation of public schools and in influence over who is appointed to the board of education.[7] A move toward integrated governance does not mean a shift away from the public's ownership of schools and its right and responsibility to demand accountability. Regardless of the form of legal authority by which the city and its public institutions are governed, however, only an informed and available public can effectively hold its elected officials accountable. Effective integrated governance would require such an informed and available public so that appointment of school board members would be based on objective standards rather than political criteria and that public schools not be used for political patronage. Clearly this new approach to governance has its detractors. Some argue that it has too short a history in too few jurisdictions to judge its effectiveness. Whatever pattern is adopted, those in authority need to address the fact that 30 percent of Mount Vernon's students who enter high school fail to graduate in four years. City officials can no longer afford to accept the idea that traditional, twentieth century models for school governance are the only alternatives.

The Role of the Clergy

The Mount Vernon community has experienced a phenomenon that Robert Putnam describes as the *erosion of social capital*.[8] Findings lead us to believe that enhanced involvement of the religious community is vital to the restoration of rich and active public engagement in Mount Vernon. The Black church continues to be a major force in the city. In spite of some negative public perceptions of their role in recent years, religious leaders continue to be viewed by that same public as a source of legitimate community leadership. There are various approaches the religious community might consider as the Mt. Vernon's schools face re-segregation. We would like to suggest a few.

Call for a Healing of the Community

Many people involved in our research asserted that the political "blame game" with its attendant finger pointing has gone on far too long. Party politics, racial and socio-economic division, and religious fragmentation are all perceived as having slowed the process of education reform and community rejuvenation. Success in the fight for equal access was perceived as a wonderful victory for the people of Mount Vernon and for humanity. The public described how it had been an example of people cooperating and then coming together in celebration of their success. However some respondents pointed out that winning the battle for greater access to schools and equal representation on the Board of Education had not been followed up with similar efforts to preserve the unity of the newly-empowered community. The United Black Clergy did establish the Coalition for Empowerment of People of African Ancestry (CEPAA) in an effort to creatively employ the many coalitions that had worked together so effectively up to that point. However, the Coalition never served as a vehicle for uniting the entire city in support of public schools. The religious community can now play an important role in facilitating this long-overdue healing of a city fractured both by the effects of de facto segregation and by the fight for equality. The city was at its best when the clergy used its influence to create a coalition that crossed religious, racial and socio-economic lines—similar to its work during the era of civil rights struggles. Black ministers still have the standing to call for an interdenominational coalition designed to bring the entire community together for healing and a new beginning.

Expand from Promoting Advocacy to Facilitating Effective Governance

Historically, the Black clergy has effectively used the pulpit to inspire civic engagement. For example, they played a key role by working with Black and White liberals to build local branches of the NAACP and the National Urban League. They galvanized an interdenominational group to help establish the Westchester affiliate of the Christian Leadership Conference—a national organization during the Civil Rights Movement.[9] They also were responsible for building upon the hard work of VOTE

(Voices of the Electorate), a grassroots effort of multiple groups fighting for greater representation on the district's school board. Ministers used their pulpits and the might of their combined congregations to heighten community awareness of such movements and to build public momentum for their support. The religious community played an important role in the public's drive to secure access to equitable and affordable housing, integrated public schools, and equal representation—both in government and on the local school board. However, since their success in gaining access to important institutions, the Black clergy have not been as successful in transitioning residents into their new role of governance. This has resulted in a public ill-equipped to take on its role as owners of public schools and other institutions to which they successfully gained full access.

Help a Disenfranchised Public Transition into Owners of Public Institutions

We discussed in Chapter 13 that, despite its eagerness to participate in the affairs of its schools, the public is ill-equipped to play their part as owners of public schools. This is due to the lack of models from which the public can learn behaviors of ownership. The challenge facing the Black church is to move members of the disenfranchised community to become an empowered group that accepts both the privileges and responsibilities of institutional ownership. The new majority must be equipped to think critically about governing, and to make sure their goals for public schools are attained. Their standard for governance must be based on objective accountability criteria in place of the current patterns of loyalty and familiarity. For education reform to be effective, the public will need to learn how to hold their elected and appointed officials accountable—regardless of skin color, affiliation, and political or social membership. Ministers possess the influence and ability to empower their parishioners and others in the community with these skills.

One model the clergy might find to be applicable to the needs of the Mount Vernon public is the work of the Industrial Area Foundation (IAF)—an interfaith, multiracial network of community organizers with the mission of revitalizing American democracy in local communities, originally in the Southwest and beyond. It works with faith-based organizations to build and sustain important coalitions of people from all walks of life, working toward common goals.[10] This network attempts to maximize the full breadth of community diversity—pulling together parishioners of multiple religious and socio-economic backgrounds. The IAF model might be a valuable guide to the Black church as it trains good stewards to engage in civic work—equipping people in their search for the collective public good. This approach might begin to address the leadership deficit so prevalent in the city.

The Role of Public Servants Charged with Managing Public Schools

Findings from our interviews and focus groups revealed the presence of a highly committed group of professionals who manage the day-to-day operations of the district's public schools. Among the 78 people we interviewed, 22 were education specialists—teachers, school nurses, security personnel, central office administrators, and school principals. They represented 28 percent of all respondents in our study. In addition we gathered a focus group of six classroom teachers. Through their combined stories we found evidence of professionals whose aspirations for the public schools were similar to those held by the general public. The vast majority of education specialists we interviewed displayed a high regard for their profession, and cared deeply about children in the district. The way many went beyond the call of duty provided further evidence of their dedication. In spite of their dedication and commitment to education, the vast majority of education specialists we interviewed had no clear understanding of the role of the public in its relationship with public schools.

Our teacher focus group provided keen insight into school culture in the district and the degree to which there is blatant resistance to the idea of public ownership of its public schools. For example, we found rich data which showed how this hostile school culture within the district is manifested at the building level. Public ownership there was, at best, conditional. If parents behaved in a way dictated by the principal, they were granted the privileges of ownership. If parents did not behave in that way, ownership and access were withheld. The issue of ownership extending beyond parents to the community-at-large was echoed as an afterthought. There was no strong evidence to suggest that the public, other than parents, were recognized as legitimate owners of public schools.

This flawed understanding of the relationships among education specialists, school board officials, and the public, would be analogous to a corporation in which the CEO's relationship to the board of directors is understood by neither party. In a properly run organization, the CEO and his or her staff are recognized as qualified experts responsible for day-to-day operations. Similarly, CEOs expect their boards not to micromanage or interfere in such routine matters. The CEO is the one in charge but clearly remains accountable to the corporate board. It is appropriate for a board to have some knowledge of the corporate business world, but the absence of such knowledge does not nullify the reporting relationship. The CEO reports to the board—period! Some will make the argument that since the Mount Vernon board of trustees represents the public, the superintendent should regard the board as the voice of the public. In theory, this principle is true, but in Mount Vernon the facts showed a huge disconnect between the board and the public; the board either did not understand, or, although understanding it, failed to follow the will of the public. To exacerbate the problem, the public was equally unaware of its ownership role. Although only 19 percent of all stakeholders understood the role of the public, a still smaller group—3 percent of the Community-at-Large stakeholder group—understood it; most didn't have a clue! This stakeholder group represents the public with no official relationship to the district. Our findings lead us to suggest that leadership needs to emerge from the office of the superintendent that will create an environment in which a paradigm shift in the culture can occur—one that allows for the realignment of the relationship between the public—the legitimate owners of public schools—and education specialists who are paid public servants appointed as caretakers for those institutions that belong to the public.

A model that the office of the superintendent might want to emulate is that of the Hartford, Connecticut Public School District. In 2006, after that district had gone through a series of failed, and/or unsustained education reform movements, Dr. Steven Adamowski became superintendent. That district was reported to have the largest achievement gap in the nation. Efforts at education reform there had never survived the tenures of their initiating superintendents. What is interesting and unique about Adamowski's approach—something that might be of value to the Mount Vernon community—was his leadership in setting the stage for sustained reform. Recognizing the important role of civic engagement in the process of guiding long-term systemic change, Adamowksi went to the business community and called for financial support for the revamping of its local education foundation—one which is closely linked to the mission of its national affiliate, the Public Education Network (PEN)—a network that seeks to build public support for public schools nationwide. Through its more than 83 Local Education Funds (LEFs), PEN is at work in 34 states, the District of Columbia, and Puerto Rico, and has an active presence in the Philippines and South Africa. It raises an estimated 200 million dollars annually to improve public schools and increase student achievement, 4 billion for quality public education, and 1.5 billion to enhance quality of instruction. It has served as a valuable tool for educating the public as to its role as owners of public education and has revitalized civic engagement by building meaningful partnerships among local school districts, businesses, government, and the public at large. In 2008 a PEN affiliate was established not far from Mt. Vernon—in Yonkers, New York. Today the LEF is active in schools throughout that district.[11]

Adamowksi recognized that the only way for his vision for public schools to be sustained after his tenure as superintendent would be through sustained public support. The business community responded to Adamowski's call for the revitalization of its local education funding with a multi-million-dollar commitment, payable over three years. Thus *Achieve Hartford!* was newly empowered in 2009. Although in its infancy, the organization is positioned to become a valuable resource for the community by providing educational information on public schools, creating forums for discussion, and serving as a critical friend to the school district. If successful, this approach will help reset the relationship between the public and those public servants elected and appointed to safeguard the public's interest.

This type of leadership from the office of the superintendent of the Mount Vernon public schools would help calibrate the delicate balance between the school district and the public. In addition, the superintendent can set the tone for a new school culture—one which acknowledges the public—not only parents—as legitimate owners of public schools and holds staff accountable to act on this recognition.

A Role for the Public

Our findings revealed the virtual absence of two major groups: the Black and White middle-class members of Mount Vernon's *bedroom* community, and members of the poor and working class. The middle class is viewed as having abandoned Mount Vernon public schools, by choosing alternative school settings for their children. The working-class and poor are viewed as caring deeply about public schools, but comprising many single parents, most working multiple jobs and juggling important priorities. Education is important to them. But in the context of what they face, education slips to the bottom of their list. These two groups are divorced from the business of public education. Consequently they make even lower the turnout rate for school board elections—typically about 6 percent.

Thomas Jefferson had it right when he said that an educated public is of the greatest value to America's democracy. Democracy cannot be sustained without an available public with a passion for self-government. None of the education reform we have called for in Mount Vernon can be achieved without the active engagement of the public. Every leadership strategy we have proposed requires public engagement at every juncture. In order to produce and sustain high-performing schools, the entire community—not just parents of children attending public schools—will have to take a greater role as owners of public education. Regardless of the economic situation, greater involvement in local school policies is of overriding importance. Education reform will occur when the new majority comes into its own and exercises its rights and responsibilities as owners of its public schools.

Epilogue

The Unresolved Issue of Ownership

The power to establish and control its schools has historically belonged to the American public. Schools were established by the public and paid for in part with public dollars. They were intended to prepare children for their rightful place in a democratic society. Yet, the history of segregated public schools in the South and what they did not achieve for the mass of African Americans who were subjected to separate and unequal public education has had a legacy of its own. For African Americans, the issue of ownership of public schools was not at the forefront in the struggles for civil rights under the U.S. Constitution. The fight for civil rights and the end of government-sponsored segregation did not focus on right of "ownership" of the educational system for African Americans, but on the right to have "access" to an equitable educational system, which the Black community had been systematically denied.

Yet this legacy of segregated public schools also includes a rich history of successful schools—public and private—that were run, for the most part, by early Black scholars who had a free hand in operating them. At the time, these schools were typically for "negro" or "colored" children and sidelined by White-dominated school boards. Nonetheless, Black academicians from some of the top universities in the country seized the opportunity to turn these schools into schools of excellence, learning institutions unparalleled on the national and regional levels.[1]

From fighting for the right to be acknowledged as part of the human race in America to the right to integrated public schools to the right to vote, the battle has historically been around access to a system to which

African Americans never belonged. Thus, the issue of ownership of public schools among African Americans has yet to be fully addressed. As re-segregation comes to America's urban centers, there will increasingly be communities like Mount Vernon where the political balance shifts and the emergence of a new *majority* prevails. This new majority will be comprised of groups historically recognized as minorities. If these new majorities are to take a leadership role in American public education, the issue of ownership must be resolved—in terms of how we view ourselves and how we are viewed by the people we appoint and elect to serve us.

Every major education reform in America has come about as a result of everyday people standing together to demand their rightful place as *owners* of America's public institutions. During the eighteenth century, a newly independent public, faced with the tasks of founding a new republic and carving out a frontier, started schools and claimed the right to maintain local control over education as a fundamental institution of democracy. In the nineteenth century, a public comprised of urban wage earners came together in a movement that fought against child labor and led to the establishment of universal education—that is, the right to a public education for children regardless of their gender or family background. During the twentieth century, a public comprised of people of diverse races and political and religious affiliations came together in the Civil Rights Movement and fought for the removal of racial barriers to public education and for the end of locally sanctioned segregated schools that barred African Americans from access to a quality public education. When faced with challenges, the American public has shown a buoyant spirit and a tenacity to rebound as guardians of education and to reclaim ownership of public schools.

In the early twenty-first century, we find signs of this buoyant spirit in Mount Vernon, New York, particularly with regard to issues affecting youth. In May 2007, following the murders of two young men in Mount Vernon, Mayor Earnest D. Davis admonished residents who were attending a town meeting to find ways to reduce violent crime, and to take a role in tackling problems, declaring, "What we're lacking here is spirit and foundation."[2] The growing rate of violent crime revived several existing groups and led to the creation of new ones, such as the Mothers of Mount Vernon (MOMs), a grassroots group comprised of family members of the murder victims. MOMs took up the cause of preventing gun violence and reducing youth and gang-related violence following the murders of eleven Mount Vernon youths in 2008. At a forum to address these issues, which was attended by over 130 people in September 2009, MOMs attributed the causes of youth and gang-related violence to the breakdown of educational resources at the middle school and high school levels in Mount Vernon, high poverty and unemployment rates, and inadequate recreational resources and programs for Mount Vernon's youth.[3]

A collateral effort was subsequently launched by the Peace Keepers from the Grace Baptist Church in early 2010. Comprised of 200 men from all walks of life who stepped forward in response to youth violence, the Peace Keepers demonstrate a readiness to take ownership of this issue. Every Saturday, approximately fifty men show up clad in orange, a symbol of solidarity, and walk the streets of some of the most challenging neighborhoods in the city. These men talk to the youth about the importance of education and share their personal stories to let young people know that success is within their reach. During the early stages of its development, leaders of this group made the deliberate decision to not pursue funding from outside sources. It was important to them to take full ownership of their work by raising seed monies from the community and self-imposed dues from their membership. The United Black Clergy raised an estimated $20,000 in seed monies.[4]

Despite the call for improved educational resources and increased programs for youth, a referendum on the Mount Vernon school budget in the spring of 2008 was defeated a second time, a process in which fewer than 6 percent of registered voters participated. As in many financially strapped urban school districts, the superintendent faced difficult choices for reducing administrative and program expenses for the 2008-2009 school year, including a 6 percent reduction in district staff and a reduction in pre-kindergarten slots. In addition, the superintendent proposed to eliminate $1.1 million for the interscholastic athletic program, thereby cancelling the season for the popular Mount Vernon Knights high school football team.[5]

Having won several state championships for the district, and served as a pathway out of poverty for several students, the Knights were the *jewel* of the MVSD, and the athletic program was something the public proudly claimed as *its own*. Thus, Mayor Clinton I. Young, who had campaigned for closer ties with the MVSD, exercised leadership in calling for the community to rally around this issue. He challenged the Mount Vernon Education Foundation to organize a fundraising drive for the $1.1 million needed to reinstate the athletic program.

The Mount Vernon Education Foundation took the lead in fundraising through a community partnership between the Foundation, the MVSD, the Office of the Mayor, and the community at large. Mount Vernon's plight became the center of national attention as people from all walks of life, near and far, responded to the challenge. From Denzel Washington, a former Mount Vernon resident, and Ben Gordon, a member of the Chicago Bulls and a former Mount Vernon high school athlete, to a couple that requested donations for the MVSD in lieu of wedding gifts, organizations, politicians, and families came together to raise the money needed to reinstate the school athletic program. Student athletes along with their coaches raised over $19,000 in one weekend by targeting motorists to contribute to the "Fill the Cooler Campaign." Together, they raised more than $1.1 million in less than eight months, $55,000 of which came from local contributions.

It can be argued that the local contribution was small. Its significance lay in demonstrating that when leadership comes from within, the public understands its role as *owners* of public education, and the public will form the coalitions needed to ensure its viability. In this case, it was the sports program: the public claimed it, took ownership of it, and accepted the responsibility to ensure its sustainability. They successfully built the coalitions needed to preserve this program for the youth. The local dollar amount was a small portion of the total, but the effort brought the entire Mount Vernon community together in support of its public schools.

Mount Vernon's experience also illustrates how the process of education reform is both fragile and complex. Overcoming legal barriers to racial inequality does not necessarily clear the path for immediate reforms at the community level. In communities where re-segregation is reshaping the political balance, much work is needed to prepare the public and its leaders for their roles as guardians of the community's public institutions. Several issues within the public domain need to be addressed before public ownership of public schools can take hold in Black-led communities. These include helping the public to build a system that benefits all children, rather than simply to manage a broken educational system. Another challenge involves nurturing a public that is representative of all social and economic and cultural groups, and has a shared vision for public education. In addition, it is necessary to equip the local public with the essential skills and wisdom needed to sustain its vision for public schools. To accomplish these tasks, the public also needs the moral strength and guidance of its various local religious institutions that have historically served as the voices of the people in the community and as teachers of non-violence.

As society moves further into the information age, much is being done among private, government, and not-for-profit sectors to become strategically positioned to respond to the technical challenges and opportunities of the twenty-first century. Similarly, the public—particularly in urban communities like Mount Vernon where a Black-led new majority has emerged—must move into the new role of rebuilding public institutions and holding themselves, as well as the people they elect, accountable for high-performing public schools.

Will this new majority make the transition to full ownership of public schools and deliver on America's promise? Or will it simply perpetuate the status quo? This is the challenge for the new majority in Mount Vernon, who once fought so hard to gain greater representation at the policymaking level.

The response to this challenge does not and cannot reside with the Board of Education alone. Although recent responses to violence and to threatened athletic programs provide some hope for nurturing ownership, a sense of skepticism lingers. One respondent points out how the potential for empowerment is great, but members of the community have not fully mastered the system or begun to embrace the power that they hold. As a result, the ability of parents to sustain a sense of ownership is tenuous, if not missing, leaving the board in isolation.

> If parents only knew the power that they have. It's interesting because, once in awhile, you see that happening and I just want to share an example. We were pressured for funding and one thing [the board] . . . decided to do . . . was to close down a program at the high school level. It was an evening program for children with special needs, and their parents came to that following meeting, all of them, and they expressed why [the board] . . . shouldn't close that program and [the board] . . . literally had to go back and reinstate the program. That's the power that parents have, you know, and unfortunately we only see it in moments of crisis. But if [parents] . . . were able to use that strength and, to the advantage of benefiting all of the schools, decide what kind of education they want and how the schools are going to be run—that's the power that communities, you know, parents have. I don't see that here at all.

More than a few voices within the MVSD defy this skepticism. In their own idiom, parents understand that because their children are not isolated, ownership of public schools requires families to overcome their own isolation from the school system. They understand ownership of public schools as a civic virtue—as a communal value—and as a choice to be embraced by adults on behalf of all children in their community. In the words of one parent, ownership of public schools is the essence of empowerment:

> Who owns the school? I own it—as a parent and as a citizen—Me. I think every parent and adult has to say "Me," because, let me tell you, if I don't own it, you know what I'm gonna say? I'm gonna say "They"—which means, "I'm powerless, that's not my fault, and there's nothing I can do about it. I'm just a victim."—But I don't believe that.
>
> I believe that if I want to make things better for my kids, I can't say, "You know, I'm just gonna be concerned with their environment and work with them and put them in the best situations" . . . because they don't live in a vacuum. They have to cross paths and interact with everybody in this community. And when I stop doing for other kids in this community, I've stopped making it a better community for my kids. Okay?
>
> You can't protect your family unless you help everybody—because there's gonna be somebody who may feel disenfranchised in some way, whether right, wrong, or indifferent. There's gonna be some void in their lives that they're gonna fill off your kids. So, if I really love my kids, and if I really wanna do the best for them, I'm gonna help other kids. Now, if I didn't have a kid, if I didn't have kids personally, I would still do it.

As newcomers to ownership, the parents and adults who comprise the new majority must ready themselves for ownership of local public schools by overcoming their isolation. Their children's future depends upon it. The educational resources needed for children to overcome the disadvantages they inherit by virtue of living in impoverished communities must come from within the community. It needs to come by way of a renewed public—positioned as owners of public schools—who have the capacity to build coalitions. It will take the development of local coalitions to demand the resources needed to address critical issues facing schools in their communities.

Urban school reform needs to look beyond such things as pedagogical innovations at the school level, new management practices, or new models of professional development for educators. Sustained reform in urban public school districts must be approached through the mobilization of its citizenry with an emphasis on a rebalancing of political power. For this to occur, the public must be prepared to accept its role as owners of public schools and engage in a collective response to the educational challenges within its community.

Why is this paramount to the future of public schools in urban communities in the twenty-first century? Because the twentieth century model of de facto segregation is obsolete and African Americans and Latinos no longer represent small numbers of marginalized groups confined to segregated neighborhoods designated for "minorities." With the demographic shifts taking place in our nation, new majorities will continue to emerge in urban municipalities across the country. Thus, it is up to these new majorities to position themselves as owners of public schools and to build and maintain the coalitions needed to hold their elected officials and administrators accountable for revitalizing public schools. Who owns public schools? I own it; we all own it!

Notes

Preface

1. For expanded treatment of this topic, See J. Henig, and W. C. Rich (Eds.), *Mayors in the Middle: Politics, Race and Mayoral Control of Urban Schools* (Princeton: Princeton University Press, 2004).

2. Fernanda Santos, "Voices Rise in Mount Vernon Over How to Fight Crime," *New York Times*, May 4, 2007. http://query.nytimes.com/gst/ fullpage.html?res=9E01E2DD113EF937A35756C0A9619C8B63&pagewanted=allpp (accessed December 12, 2010)

Introduction

1. David Mathews, *Reclaiming Public Education by Reclaiming Our Democracy*, (Dayton, OH: The Kettering Foundation Press, 2006), vi.

2. Mathews, *Reclaiming*.

3. G. Orfield, *Schools More Separate: Consequences of a Decade of Desegregation* (Cambridge, MA: Harvard University, The Civil Rights Project 2001).

4. C. N. Stone, et al., *Building Civic Capacity: The Politics of Reforming Urban Schools* (Lawrence, KS: University Press of Kansas, 2001).

5. Stone, *Civic Capacity*, 20.

6. H. C. Giles, "Parent Engagement as a Social Reform Strategy" (*Digest: Eric Clearinghouse on Urban Education,* May, 1998, ISSN0889 8049), *135*. Retrieved January 31, 2007, from http://iume.tc.columbia.edu/eric_archive.asp?show=1

7. C. Vincent, *Parents and Teachers: Power and Participation* (London: Falmer Press, 1996).

8. W. Friedman, A. Gutnick, and J. Danzberger, *Public Engagement in Education* (New York: Public Agenda, 1999).

9. R. Putnam, *Bowling Alone: The Collapse and Revival of American Community* (New York: Simon and Schuster, 2000).

10. David Mathews, *Why Public Schools? Whose Public Schools? What Early Communities Have to Tell Us*, "Stories from Early Alabama (Montgomery, AL: NewSouth Books, 2001).

11. J. Salmond, *My Mind Set on Freedom: A History of the Civil Rights Movement, 1954-1968* (Chicago: Ivan R. Dee, 1997).

12. The literature is rich with perspectives on the civic capacity of a community to support quality education by drawing from the political power that has historically resonated from the collective will of the people. *See* C. N. Stone, "Civic Capacity: What, Why and From Whence?" in *The Public Schools*, S. Fuhrman and M. Lazerson, eds., 209-234 (New York: Oxford University Press, 2005). See also Mathews (2001, 2006), Puriefoy (2005), and Stone (1998).

In addition, see A. R. Broun, W. D. Puriefoy and E. Richard. *Public Engagement in School Reform: Building Public Responsibility for Public Education* (Washington, DC: 2006)

Chapter 1: Themes of Public Engagement in Historical Perspective

1. See, for example, Addis (2003), Francois (2004), Harris (1938), Hayes (2006), and Mathews (2001).

2. David Mathews, *Why Public Schools? Whose Public Schools? What Early Communities Have to Tell Us*, "Stories from Early Alabama (Montgomery, AL: NewSouth Books, 2001).

3. Ibid.

4. Ibid.

5. Ibid.

6. Ibid.

7. Ibid.

8. E. P. Cubberley, *Public Education in the United States: A Study and Interpretation of American Educational History* (Cambridge, MA: Riverside Press, 1919).

9. Cubberley, *Public Education ... A Study*, 12.

10. Cubberley, *Public Education ... A Study*.

11. C. F. Kaestle, *Pillars of the Republic: Common Schools and American Society, 1780–1860* (New York: Hill and Wang, 1983).

12. Kaestle, *Pillars* (1983).

13. D. Mathews, *Politics for People*, 2nd ed. (Chicago: University of Illinois Press, 1999).

14. C. F. Kaestle, "The Common School" in *The Story of American Public Education,* S. Mondale and S. B. Patton (Eds.), 11-17 (Boston: Beacon Press, 2001).

15. L. A. Cremin, The *American Common School: An Historical Conception* (NY: Bureau of Publications, Teachers College, Columbia University, 1951).

16. Kaestle, "The Common School," 11–17.

17. Mathews, *Politics for People.*

18. V. T. Thayer, *Formative Ideas in American Education: From the Colonial Period to the Present* (New York: Dodd, Mead and Company, 1965).

19. H. Harris, *American Labor* (New Haven: Yale University Press, 1938).

20. Ibid., 18.

21. Harris, *American Labor.*

22. Ibid., 20.

23. J. Spring, *The American School: 1642–1993*, Third Edition (New York: McGraw-Hill, 1994).

24. Harris, *American Labor.*

25. Spring, *American School.*

26. J. Williams, "The Ruling that Changed America," Introduction to *Brown v. Board of Education: Its Impact on Public Education 1954–2004*, D. Byrne, (Ed.), 21-28 (New York: Word for Word Publishing, 2005).

Chapter 2: The Elusiveness of Education Reform

1. M. W. McLaughlin, M. A. Irby, and J. Langman, *Urban Sanctuaries: Neighborhood Organizations in the Lives and Futures of Inner-city Youth* (San Francisco: Jossey-Bass, 2001),

2. C. N. Stone, J. R. Henig, B. D. Jones, and C. Pierannunzi, *Building Civic Capacity: The Politics of Reforming Urban Schools* (Lawrence, KS: University Press of Kansas, 2001).

3. G. Orfield and C. Lee, *Racial Transformation and the Changing Nature of Segregation* (Cambridge, MA: The Civil Rights Law Project, Harvard University, 2006).

4. J. R. Henig and W. C. Rich, "Mayor-centrism in Context," in *Mayors in the Middle: Politics, Race and Mayoral Control of Urban Schools*, J. Henig, and W. C. Rich (eds.), 3-24. (Princeton, NJ: Princeton University Press, 2004).

5. Orfield and Lee, *Racial Transformation* (2006).

6. Ibid.

7. Ibid.

8. J. Kozol, *The Shame of the Nation: The Restoration of Apartheid Schooling in America* (New York: Crown Publishers, 2005).

9. Ibid.

10. Ibid.

11. G. Orfield, *Schools More Separate: Consequences of a Decade of Desegregation* (Cambridge, MA: The Civil Rights Project, Harvard University, 2001).

12. The trends are based on NCES Common Core of Data for 2000 to 2001, containing data submitted by all U.S. schools to the Department of Education. E. Frankenberg, et al., *Multiracial Society with Segregated Schools: Are We Losing the Dream?* Report No. UD 035 435 (Cambridge, MA: Harvard University, The Civil Rights Project, 2003). ERIC Document Reproduction Service No. ED 472 347.

13. Orfield and Lee, *Racial Transformation* (2006).

14. Ibid.

15. Orfield, *Schools More Separate* (2001).

16. J. R. Henig, and W. C. Rich (Eds.), *Mayors in the Middle*, 2004).

17. J. R. Henig, et al., *The Color of School Reform: Race, Politics, and the Challenge of Urban Education* (Princeton, NJ: Princeton University Press, 1999).

18. Henig, et al., *Color of School Reform.*

19. Ibid.

Chapter 3: The Evolution of a Black-led City

1. The historical material in this chapter is adapted with permission from L. H. Spruill, *A Time to Remember: A Portrait of African-American Life in Mount Vernon* (Mount Vernon, NY: Afro-American Workshop, 1993). The author draws from original documents to trace the history of the African American community in Mount Vernon, New York. It is the only published history of the African American community in Mount Vernon known to this author.

Chapter 4: The Mount Vernon School District in 2007

1. Westchester County Department of Planning, *Databook: Westchester County* (White Plains, New York: 2005).

2. E. Brenner, "4 Line Up to Succeed Mount Vernon Mayor," *New York Times,* October 8, 1995, [Electronic Version]. Retrieved April 11, 2007, from http://query.nytimes.com/gst/fullpage.html?res=9E0DE2D91239F93BA35753C1A963958260&scp=1&sq=four+line +up+mount+vernon+mayor&st=nyt

3. *Databook.*

4. American Community Survey 2005. *Data Profile Highlights.* Retrieved on April 12, 2007, from http://factfinder.census.gov/servlet/ACSSAFFFacts?_event=SEARCH&GEO_id=16000US365

5. Westchester County Department of Social Services and Westchester County Youth Bureau, *2004–2005 Needs assessment: Supplement to the Child and Family Service Plan,* New York: (2005).

6. New York State Department of Education, *New York State District Report Card: Accountability and overview report for the Mount Vernon City School District* (Albany, NY: 2008).

7. D. Censor, "Our Annual Public High School Report Card," *Westchester Magazine* April 2007, 78–85.

8. New York State Department of Education *District Report Card.*

9. The two lowest performing districts were Yonkers and Peekskill in 2002–2003. Westchester County Department of Social Services and Westchester County Youth Bureau (2005).

10. New York State Department of Education. (2008)

Chapter 9: Major Problems Facing the District

1. Mount Vernon City School District (2008). *Employee Ethnic Distribution.* Unpublished manuscript.

Chapter 18: Causes for Disenfranchisement

1. *See* J. Henig and W. C. Rich (eds.), *Mayors in the Middle: Politics, Race and Mayoral Control of Urban Schools* (Princeton, NJ: Princeton University Press, 2004).

2. Parallels can be drawn between Mount Vernon's African Americans in their battle with the members of the ICA in the 1970s and 1980s and Freire's theory of oppression based on the struggle of the oppressed in Brazil. In essence, the behaviors of the new Black political power base took on the characteristics of the oppressor, a phenomenon Freire cautions the oppressed to avoid. This is very difficult to achieve in that once the oppressed overcome the oppressor, they have no other model from which to emulate behavior except that which had been provided by the oppressor. Freire helps us put into context the cyclical pattern of behavior taking place among the leadership in Mount Vernon and how it has delayed the public's building a public school system based on the principles of humanity. P. Freire, *Pedagogy of the Oppressed* (New York: The Continuum Publishing Group, 2005).

Chapter 19:
The Role of Black Churches

1. For example, in the 2009 elections, Bishop Collie Nathan Edwers, pastor of the Friendship Worship Center and an officer of the United Black Clergy, lost his bid for a seat on the Mount Vernon City Council. He was defeated in spite of having the endorsement of the United Black Clergy.

2. A discussion of organizational cultures and the art of forming coalitions with unlikely groups, for the purpose of achieving some other important objectives, is found in L. G. Bolman and T. E. Deal, *Reframing Organizations: Artistry, Choice and Leadership*, (San Francisco: Jossey-Bass, 2008).

Chapter 20:
A New Beginning for Building Public Support for Public Schools

1. J. R. Henig, W. C. Rich, "Mayor-Centrism in Context," in J. Henig and W. Rich, (Eds.) *Mayors in the Middle: Politics, Race and Mayoral Control of Urban Schools* (Princeton: Princeton University Press, 2004). M. Orr, "The Limits of Mayor Control," in *Mayors in the Middle: Politics, Race and Mayor Control of Urban Schools* (Princeton: Princeton University Press, 2004), 3-24.

2. Henig and Rich, "Mayor-Centrism in Context."

3. K. K. Wong, F. X. Shen, D. S. Anagnostopoulos and S. Rutledge, *The Education Mayor: Improving America's Schools* (Washington, DC: Georgetown University Press, 2007).

4. Henig and Rich, "Mayor-Centrism in Context."

5. J. Henig, "Washington, D. C: Race, Issue Definition, and School Board Restructuring," in *Mayors in the Middle: Politics, Race and Mayor Control of Urban Schools*. J. Henig, and W. C. Rich (eds) (Princeton, NJ: Princeton University, 2004).

6. Wong, et al., *The Education Mayor*.

7. There are several approaches to granting authority to the mayor. For example the appointing of school board trustees could be limited. The governing authority could have sunset provisions. See Wong, et al., *The Education Mayor* for a full description of alternative approaches to imposing an integrated governance model.

8. R. Putnam, *Bowling Alone: The Collapse and Revival of American Community*. (New York: Simon and Schuster, 2000).

9. L. Spruill, *A Time to Remember: A Portrait of African-American Life in Mount Vernon* (Mount Vernon, NY: Afro-American Workshop, 1993).

10. M. R. Warren. *Dry Bones Rattling: Community Building to Revitalize American Democracy* (Princeton: Princeton University Press, 2001). Also see D. Shirley, *Community Organizing for Urban School Reform* (Austin, TX: University Texas Press, 1997).

11. See Public Education Network/*Education Week* National Survey of Public Opinion 2002. *Accountability for All: What Voters Want from Education Candidates*. http://www.publiceducation.org/pdf/Publications/National_Poll/April_2002_Full_Report.pdf (accessed on Feb 15, 2007).

Epilogue: The Unresolved Issue of Ownership

1. *See*: S. Walker, *Their Highest Potential* (Chapel Hill, NC: University of North Carolina Press, 1996) and T. Sowell, "Patterns of Black Excellence" *Public Interest,* (43) Spring 1976, 26-58.

2. F. Santos, and A. Gruen, "Voices Rise in Mount Vernon Over How to Fight Crime," *New York Times*, May 4, 2007.

3. Interview with Chanelle Hyde, founder of *Mothers Who Have Lost Children to Violence in Mount Vernon*, August, 28, 2010.

4. Interview with Mount Vernon City Councilman Yuhanna Edwards, August 27, 2010.

5. W. Hu, "For Many Student Athletes, Game Over," *The New York Times*, July 28, 2008. http://www.nytimes.com/2008/07/28/education/28sports.html (accessed Oct 22, 2010).

References

Addis, C. *Jefferson's Vision for Education, 1760–1845*. New York: Peter Lang Publishing, 2003.

American Community Survey 2005. *Data Profile Highlights*. Retrieved on April 12, 2007, from http://factfinder.census.gov/servlet/ACSSAFFFacts?_event=SEARCH&GEO_id=16000US365

Bolman, L. G. and T. E. Deal. *Reframing Organizations: Artistry, Choice and Leadership*. San Francisco: Jossey-Bass, 2008.

Brenner, E. "4 Line Up to Succeed Mount Vernon Mayor." *New York Times,* October 8, 1995. [Electronic Version]. Retrieved April 11, 2007, from http://query.nytimes.com/gst/fullpage.html?res=9E0DE2D91239F93BA35753C1A963958260&scp=1&sq=four+line+up+mount+vernon+mayor&st=nyt

Broun, A. R., W. D. Puriefoy, and W. Richard. *Public Engagement in School Reform: Building Public Responsibility for Public Education.* Unpublished manuscript, 2006.

Censor, D. "Our Annual Public High School Report Card." *Westchester Magazine*, April 2007.

Cremin, L. A. *The American Common School: An Historical Conception* (NY: Bureau of Publications, Teachers College, Columbia University, 1951).

Cubberly, E. P. *Public Education in the United States A Study and Interpretation of American Educational History*. Cambridge, MA: The Riverside Press, 1919.

Francois, R. J. *The Rise and Fall of American Public Schools: The Political Economy of Public Education in the Twentieth Century.* Westport, CT: Praeger Publishers, 2004.

Frankenberg, E., C. Lee, and G. Orfield. *Multiracial Society with Segregated Schools: Are We Losing the Dream?* (Report No. UD035

435). Cambridge, MA: Harvard University, 2003. (ERIC Document Reproduction Service No. ED472347)

Freire, P. *Pedagogy of the Oppressed.* New York: The Continuum Publishing Group, 2005.

Friedman, W., A. Gutnick, and J. Danzberger. *Public Engagement in Education.* White paper prepared for The Ford Foundation by Public Agenda, 1999.

Giles, H. C. "Parent Engagement as a Social Reform Strategy." *Digest: Eric Clearinghouse on Urban Education, 135*, May, 1998. ISSN0889 8049. Retrieved January 31, 2007, from http://iume.tc.columbia.edu/eric_archive.asp?show=1

Hammersley, M. and P. Atkinson. *Ethnography: Principles in Practice* (2nd ed.). London: Routledge, 1995.

Hammersly, M. *What's Wrong with Ethnography?* New York: Routledge, 1992.

Harris, H. *American Labor.* New Haven, CT: Yale University Press, 1938.

Hayes, W. *Horace Mann's Vision of the Public Schools: Is It Still Relevant?* Lanham, MD: Rowman & Littlefield Education, 2006.

Henderson, A. T. and K. L. Mapp. *A New Wave of Evidence: The Impact of School Family and Community Connections on Student Achievement.* Austin, TX: Southwest Development Laboratory, 2002.

Henig, J. "Washington, D.C.: Race, Issue Definition and School Board Restructuring." In *Mayors in the Middle: Politics, Race and Mayoral Control of Urban Schools*, J. Henig, and W. C. Rich (Eds.), 191-218. Princeton, NJ: Princeton University Press, 2004.

Henig, J. R. and W. C. Rich. "Mayor-centrism in Context." In *Mayors in the Middle: Politics, Race and Mayoral Control of Urban Schools*, Henig, J. and W. C. Rich (Eds.), 3-24. Princeton, NJ: Princeton University Press, 2004.

Henig, J. R., et al. *The Color of School Reform: Race, Politics, and the Challenge of Urban Education.* Princeton, NJ: Princeton University Press, 1999.

Hu, W. "For Many Student Athletes, Game Over." *New York Times*, Education Section July 28, 2008. http://www.nytimes.com/2008/07/28/education/28sports.html?pagewanted=1&_r=3&sq=Mount%20Vernon&st=nyt&scp=1

Kaestle, C. F. *Pillars of The Republic: Common Schools and American Society, 1780–1860.* New York: Hill and Wang, 1983.

Kaestle, C. F. "The Common School." In *The Story of American Public Education,* Mondale, S. and S. B. Patton (Eds.), 11-17 . Boston: Beacon Press, 2001.

Kozol, J. *The Shame of the Nation: The Restoration of Apartheid Schooling in America.* New York: Crown Publishers, 2005.

Mathews, D. *Politics for People,* (2nd ed). Chicago: University of Illinois Press, 1999.

Mathews, D. *Why Public Schools? Whose Public Schools? What Early Communities Have to Tell Us*, "Stories from Early Alabama." Montgomery, AL: NewSouth Books, 2001.

Mathews, D. *Reclaiming Public Education by Reclaiming Our Democracy*. Dayton, OH: The Kettering Foundation Press, 2006.

McLaughlin M. W., M. A. Irby, and J. Langman. *Urban Sanctuaries: Neighborhood Organizations in the Lives and Futures of Inner-City Youth.* San Francisco: Jossey-Bass, 2001.

Mount Vernon City School District (2008). Employee Ethnic Distribution. Unpublished manuscript

New York State Department of Education. *New York State District Report Card: Accountability and Overview Report for the Mount Vernon City School District.* Albany, NY, 2008.

Orfield, G. & C. Lee. *Brown At 50: King's Dream or Plessy's Nightmare?* Cambridge, MA: The Civil Rights Law Project, Harvard University, 2004.

Orfield, G. and C. Lee, *Racial Transformation and the Changing Nature of Segregation* (Cambridge, MA: The Civil Rights Law Project, Harvard University, 2006).

Orfield, G. *Schools More Separate: Consequences of a Decade of Desegregation.* Cambridge, MA: The Civil Rights Project, Harvard University, 2001.

Orr, M. "Limits of Mayoral Control," in *Mayors in the Middle*, J. R. Henig, and W. C. Rich (Eds.), 25-58. (Princeton, NJ: Princeton University Press, 2004)

Public Education Network/*Education Week* National Survey of Public Opinion 2002. *Accountability for All: What Voters Want from Education Candidates.* Retrieved on February 15, 2007, from http://www.publiceducation.org/pdf/Publications/National_Poll/April_2002_Full_Report.pdf

Puriefoy, W. D. "The Education of Democratic Citizens: Citizen Mobilization and Public Education." In *The Public Schools*, Fuhrman, S.

and M. Lazerson (Eds.), 235-251. New York: Oxford University Press, 2005.

Putnam, R. D. *Bowling Alone: The Collapse and Revival of American Community*. New York: Simon and Schuster, 2000.

Salmond, J. A. *My Mind Set on Freedom: A History of the Civil Rights Movement, 1954-1968*. Chicago: Ivan R. Dee, 1997.

Santos, F., and A. Gruen. "Voices Rise in Mount Vernon Over How to Fight Crime." *New York Times*, May 4, 2007. http://query.nytimes.com/gst/fullpage.html?res=9E01E2DD113EF937A35756C0A9619C8B63&pagewanted=allpp.

Shirley, D. *Community Organizing for Urban School Reform*. Austin, TX: University of Texas Press, 1997.

Sowell, Thomas. "Patterns of Black Excellence." *Public Interest*. (43) Spring 1976, 26-58. http://www.nationalaffairs.com/doclib/20080527_197604302patternsofblackexcellencethomassowell.pdf

Spring, J. *The American School: 1642–1993*. (3rd ed.). New York: McGraw-Hill, 1994.

Spruill, L. H. *A Time to Remember*. Mount Vernon, NY: Afro-American Workshop, 1993.

Stone, C. N. "Civic Capacity and Urban School Reform." In *Changing Urban Education*, C. N. Stone (Ed.), 250–273. Lawrence, KS: University Press of Kansas 1998.

Stone, C. N. "Civic Capacity: What, Why, and From Whence?" In *The Public Schools*, Fuhrman, S. and M. Lazerson (Eds.), 209–234. New York: Oxford University Press, 2005.

Stone, C. N., J. R. Henig, B. D. Jones, and C. Pierannunzi. *Building Civic Capacity: The Politics of Reforming Urban Schools*. Lawrence, KS: University Press of Kansas, 2001.

Thayer, V. T. Formative Ideas in American Education: From the Colonial Period to the Present. New York: Dodd, Mead and Company, 1965.

Vincent, C. Parents and Teachers: Power and Participation. London: Falmer Press, 1996.

Walker, S. V. *Their Highest Potential. An African School Community in the Segregated South*. Chapel Hill, NC: University of North Carolina Press, 1996.

Warren, M. R. *Dry Bones Rattling: Community Building to Revitalize American Democracy*. Princeton: Princeton University Press, 2001.

Westchester County Department of Planning. *Databook: Westchester County*. White Plains, NY: 2005.

Westchester County Department of Social Services and Westchester County Youth Bureau *2004–2005 Needs Assessment: Supplement to the Child and Family Service Plan.* New York, 2005.

Williams, J. "The Ruling That Changed America" (Introduction). *Brown v. Board of Education: Its Impact on Public Education 1954–2004.* Byrne, D. (ed.), New York: Word for Word Publishing, 2005.

Wong, K. K., F. X. Shen, D. S. Anagnostopoulos, and S. Rutledge. *The Education Mayor: Improving America's Schools*. Washington, DC: Georgetown University Press, 2007.

Index

About the Author

Claudia L. Edwards has devoted her career to improving the quality of life for families throughout New York State. As an innovator in executive leadership and corporate philanthropy, she has succeeded in building public, private, and community partnerships to respond to gaps in education, health and human services, and affordable housing. She has held positions as Executive Director for the Housing and Neighborhood Development Institute in Mount Vernon; Vice President for Fund Distribution for the United Way of Westchester and Putnam; Executive Director of the Reader's Digest Foundation, and its Director of Corporate Contributions. She is the founder and president of the Education Consulting Group, which provides services to non-profit and public institutions in the areas of leadership, strategic planning, board development, and program design. She also serves as a trustee for the Westchester Medical Center and a Director for the Westchester Department of Transportation. Dr. Edwards is an Assistant Professor in the EdD Program in Executive Leadership at St. John Fisher College at the College of New Rochelle. She holds a PhD from the Graduate School of Education at Fordham University and a Master of Urban Planning degree from the Robert F. Wagner School of Public Service at New York University. She is recognized as a Distinguished Alumna of the State University of New York at Purchase and Bronx Community College.